The Quest for the Original Horse Whisperers

RUSSELL LYON

Luath Press Limited

EDINBURGH

www.luath.co.uk

First Published 2003
Reprinted 2003

The paper used in this book is recyclable. It is made from low
chlorine pulps produced in a low energy, low emission manner
from renewable forests.

Printed and bound by
Creative Print & Design, Ebbw Vale

Typeset in Sabon 10.5 by Senga Fairgrieve

For Carol, Kate and Dan

Contents

Acknowledgements

I am greatly indebted to a large number of people for generous help and encouragement while I researched for this book. I am especially grateful to all those people who contacted me via local newspapers such as the *Dundee Courier, Southern Reporter, Aberdeen Press and Journal* and the *Eastern Daily*. Their letters and photographs have been invaluable.

Letter contributors include:
Mrs Marjory MacQueen, Colin Landymore, Mary J Williamson, GR Sutherland, Mr Juby, Mr Millar from Stirling, DG Attwood, JS Steele, Douglas C Nicol, Kathleen Ager, David Grimwood, Dr Roger Leitch, Dorothy Slee, Esther Smith, Deirdre Leitch, GW Hunter, Major CW Shand, George Grey, Elizabeth Allen, Alexander Davidson, Ian MacFarlane, David Cain, Elaine Edwards, Colin Campbell, Daniel Millar, Mrs Sidell, May Ralph, L Burrows, David Currie, Stuart Gove, Bill Eddie, Betsy Verrent-Harvey, Ian Blair, James Buchanan, JA Sheridan, Ron Garson, 'Craigie' of the *Dundee Courier*, Harry Mackitosh, Ian Barr, Tommy Brown, Chris Wood, David Smith, JF Sanderson, Andre Gow, William Milne, Charles Aldred, Ray Hubbard, Kathryn Jackson, Cormack M Sinclair, William McLay.

Photographs were contributed by:
Mrs DH Turner, Betty Barron, Rosemary Button, Charles Aldred, W Davie, Hilda Fairhead, David Smith, Mrs Barker, Mr Levien, John MacFarlane, Heather Garman, Phyllis Harwood, Hilda Burrows, GB Mills, GW Mallinson, L Burrows, DF Clarry, RW Shaw, W Bryce, C Greves, H Garman, G Middler, Jesse Scott, Mrs Diane and Miss Elizabeth Bullard.

I would like especially to thank Elaine Edwards of the Royal Museum and the Country Life Archive, Dr Frances Prior, the National Museum and National Library of Scotland, the Shire, Clydesdale, Percheron and Suffolk Punch Societies; Mark Steven and Jan Byrne of BBC Radio Scotland; Catriona Scott and Justin Crozier who make editing look easy, when it is not, finally Gavin, Nele and all the staff at Luath Press for their very able and willing assistance in all the stages of production of this book and my wife Christine for her tolerance in moments of stress.

Introduction

IN THE LAST FEW YEARS great interest has been shown in the equine world in 'horse whispering', especially after the success of the novel *The Horse Whisperers* which is said to be based on the life and work of Monty Roberts, the American with a world-wide reputation for his alternative method of training young horses. At about the same time that 'Modern Whispering' came into vogue, I began my serious quest for the original horse whisperers as I had a dim memory of older methods from my childhood.

I was born and brought up on a mixed livestock farm in the Upper Ward of Lanarkshire. One of my earliest memories is of sitting on a cart with our ploughman Jake. A Clydesdale gelding called Dick was pulling the cart and we were taking dung from the calf pens out to the field to be spread as fertiliser. There was nothing to protect us from the muck apart from a thick hessian sack which could not prevent the all-pervading smell permeating our clothes and hair. However I was impervious to everything apart from the delight of being where I was, perched high above the ground and aware of the envious glances of my sister who had not been selected for the key job of being Jake's assistant. I could not have been more than five years old at the time.

As I got older I was encouraged to lead the same massive animal backwards and forwards while he was hitched to the fork-lift that raised the huge bundles of hay on to the stacks at hay-making time. I was also allowed to accompany our horses on the short journey to the blacksmith's shop for them to be fitted with new shoes. The smoke and burning smell from their enormous hooves, as they stood placidly while red-hot shoes were fitted for size, remains with me still.

Heavy horses were so much an essential part of farm life in Scotland that their presence was taken for granted, but when the time came for them to be replaced by tractors, most farmers were only too pleased to see them go. For my part, I was as delighted as any small boy could be when in the early 1950s the last horse left, the stable was turned into a calf house and the 'little grey Fergie' arrived.

However, despite my admiration for the Ferguson tractor, my love and admiration for the heavy horse stayed with me into my professional career as a veterinary surgeon. In my private practice, which has been based almost exclusively in Cambridgeshire and Norfolk, I have handled and treated many heavy horses, mostly Shire, Percheron and Suffolk Punch. I have got to know many of the men who keep these animals mostly for show and breeding purposes, and often at great financial costs to themselves. By doing so, they have kept alive to this day the traditions of horse keeping and the heavy horse breeds.

Looking back now with the benefit of hindsight, I would say that it is highly likely that our ploughman Jake, who could certainly tell a good story, was a member of the secret Society of Horsemen, one of the original horse whisperers, and also a Mason; he is certainly the source of my interest in horse whispering.

This led me to research in many places, from the Scottish Museum of Agriculture to the Royal Museum and the National Library of Scotland, and to visit different locations. I spoke to many people in both Scotland and England. In addition, I wrote to all the regional newspapers in Scotland and East Anglia asking for assistance and memories from their readers and I was astonished by the response. A great many letters were received from old whisperers and from their sons and daughters and grandsons and granddaughters, not only in this country but also in Canada, Australia, the United States and New Zealand. I have been sent copies of hand-written notebooks of oaths, old remedies, cures and observations. Many old photographs also came my way, as well as two tapes made by very old men telling of their life with heavy horses.

To say I am indebted to them all would be to understate their contribution to my quest and this book. Without their help it would hardly have been possible. There are very few horsemen alive who can still remember the halcyon days of the heavy horse, and I felt it was important to record as much information as possible before it was lost forever. I hope this book will do justice to their collective memories.

Folk memories can take a long time to die as I was reminded just the other day. I was in a pub in Welney (a quiet little village in Norfolk) with a client who is an old friend. I was explaining to him something of my quest over the last two years and was surprised to discover how much he knew about 'whispering' and the 'Frog's Bone Ritual'. He had learnt all about it as a youth from the old horsemen who used to frequent The Lamb and Flag. After a few too many pints of Adnams or Greene King IPA, they would tell the old stories, doubtless much embellished by time and beer, to any young impressionable lad who cared to listen. There is little doubt that, despite the oath of secrecy taken by all members of the Society of Horsemen, this is how much of the traditions and memories of the old whisperers were handed down.

Russell Lyon
May 2003

CHAPTER ONE

How It All Began

THE ORIGINS OF THE Secret Society of Horsemen – the original horse whisperers – which first came to prominence in rural communities of northern and eastern Scotland in the late 18th and early 19th centuries lay in the unique relationship and rapport that men had with the horses which they worked. In most instances on a working farm of that time, men and animals virtually lived together, certainly sharing a roof and usually with only a thin partition separating human and animal quarters. Close bonds with horses were not unique to ploughmen. Over thousands of years, whether in warfare or at work, men who had demonstrated a knowledge and skill in handling horses lived very closely with their animals and were greatly valued by the society of their time. Their knowledge, skill and mythology were handed down mostly by word of mouth from generation to generation.

It is generally accepted that horses were first domesticated about 8,000 years ago. The tarpan, the wild horse (now extinct) from the steppes of eastern Europe, is believed to have been the first equine to be tamed by man. The evidence for this has been obtained from archaeological digs in southern Russia and the Ukraine, mostly around the area of the Caspian Sea. Horses had been hunted in the wild for meat until someone realised how much more convenient it would be to catch and tame them and keep them as a convenient source of food. It is difficult to establish when the transition was made to taming the horse to use as a pack animal. There is little doubt that donkeys were first used for this purpose since, being smaller, they would have been easier to catch, handle and domesticate.

Domesticated horses do not appear in any number in Northern or Central Europe until around 2000 BC and it is certain that their usefulness as beasts of burden greatly contributed to the rise of civilisation and the growth of trade. The use of carts and chariots developed on the steppes and then spread to Europe.

The culture and mythology concerning the horse, as well as practical experience and expertise, spread with its movement into western Europe. It was once thought that the first people to use horses in the British Isles – the Celts – moved with their horses in a westward drift from eastern and central Europe, but archaeologists have in the last ten years disproved this. 'Celts' was another name for the Iron Age people of northern Europe and they were not involved in mass migration. It is now thought that methods of horse training and control which originated in Persia (Iran), Egypt and Greece spread with the increase in trade. The Greeks were especially skilled in horse handling and were employed by the Romans to assist them in the care and treatment of their horses.

The early equestrians used nose rings, very similar to those still used to control bulls, before mouth bits were invented. Lip rings had a similar function. The first saddles to be recognisable as such came into being around the 4th century AD. Stirrups appeared when Asian horsemen sewed loops of leather on to saddlecloths in order to support their legs during long journeys. Attila the Hun introduced them into Europe in the 5th century AD, but they were not in general use in western Europe until the 9th century.

* * *

The Society of Horsemen which originated in north-east Scotland had its heyday between 1850 and 1930. The roots of the Society are obscure, but they are thought by many, including members, to go back to pagan times. Evidence for this might be the use during Society meetings of Greek names, such as Perseus, Parnassus and Apollo – all clearly from Greek mythology. However, the Scottish education system, even for working rural families, was excellent, and the original instigators of the Society may have learnt at least a smattering of Greek in school. Robert Burns, Scotland's national poet, who was born in 1759, learnt some Latin and Greek as part of his education at the insistence of his father who originated in the north-east of Scotland.

Burns, like his father, was a farmer who worked horses on a very small uneconomic farm. He was never likely to have been a member of the Society as the rules specifically excluded farmers from membership, but his sympathies would have been with the Horsemen. Burns disliked very much the social distinctions which divided the working classes from the landowners and wealthy merchants. His poem *A Man's a Man for a' That* could have been written for the Horsemen and most would have agreed with its sentiments:

Is there for honest poverty,
That hings his head, an a' that?
The coward slave, we pass him by –
We dare be poor for a' that,
Our toils obscure, an a' that,
The rank is but the guinea's stamp,
The man's the gowd for a' that!

Then let us pray that come it may,
(As come it will for a' that) –
That Sense and Worth o'er a' the earth
May bear the gree, an a' that,
For a' that, an a' that,
It's comin yet for a' that,
That man to man, the warld o'er,
Shall brithers be for a' that.

Burns was a Mason. According to many, Freemasonry had its roots in Egypt with the pharaohs and temple worship. Men who had links to Freemasonry may have carried over its mythology into the Secret Society of Horsemen. The secret rituals observed by members of the Society bear a striking resemblance to many Masonic practices, and in modern times many of the old horse societies come under the wing of the Freemasons. The Buchan Ploughmen, for instance, are now the Sons of the Soil Masonic Lodge, operating out of Aberdeen's Crown Street Temple.

The oath that initiates into the Secret Society had to take commences 'hele, conceal and never reveal'. This is an old pagan Germanic formula which probably originated with the Anglo-Saxons. It must have been passed down by tradition and word of mouth.

Over the centuries, long before the Buchan ploughmen formed their groups, the secrets of horse whispering were concealed by supposed witchcraft and black magic. In the ancient world anything that was not understood was attributed to the devil and unnatural practices. Many so-called witches were able to make a horse stand and not move as if paralysed. This ability to 'hex', 'jade' or 'stop' a horse, as it was variously called, was not confined to so-called witches. Priests were also recorded as having this skill.

A note in Gibbon's *The Decline and Fall of the Roman Empire* concerns a 6th-century Frankish king called Clovis. Clovis won a great victory on the battlefield and as a consequence presented offerings to St. Martin of Tours. Among the gifts was a highly prized war-horse. Clovis, once the heady delights of victory had faded a bit, realised he needed to get this highly-trained animal back and offered to redeem it for 100 golden pieces. When the time came to collect the beast, the horse dug its heels in and refused to leave the stable. It remained there until the offer was doubled whereupon it mysteriously walked out without any trouble at all! There is little doubt that the priest looking after the horse was using the same methods to stop the animal that were used many centuries later by ploughmen in the north-east of Scotland who were members of the Secret Society of Horsemen.

Another case, quoted by Dr Margaret Murray, was of a man sentenced to the galleys. He had stopped a horse dead in its tracks by using vervian, an extract of a plant of the genus verbena. This plant was supposed to have magic qualities, credited with efficacy in love potions and against witches. The man had felt sorry for the beast which had been galloping along a road. The 'magic' he used was that he said the Paternoster and Ave Maria five times over the vervian before he placed it on the road and the animal pulled up and would not proceed any further. The court convicted him of witchcraft although he was most likely a horse-loving Christian.

It is supposed that by late medieval times horse whispering flourished as a secret craft like that of the masons and the millers, and often in direct conflict with the more middle-class groups who formed the Merchant Guilds.

The Society of Freemasons became open to non-practising masons and this saved it from extinction, unlike the Society of Millers which guarded its secrets very jealously and would not allow anyone other than millers to join; nor would millers work with non-millers. Millers, who worked wind or water mills, were put out of business by new technology. The result was that the Millers' Society died out and its secrets died with it. The Society of Horsemen was no less secret than the Millers' Society and they were very particular about who was allowed to join, but they did not have a ban on working with non-members.

The growth of the Society of Horsemen in the 18th century was related to two factors. Until the invention of the horse collar, which doubled the pulling power of the horse, and of the efficient swing plough by James Small, most ploughing was done with a very heavy wooden plough known in many parts as the twal-owsen [twelve-oxen] plough. This was pulled either by a team of oxen or a combination of oxen and horses, and the size of the team depended on the soil. It was at least a two-man job to control and direct the team. This system was used by Robert Burns all his farm-working life. He farmed in several locations in south-west Scotland and the soil on all his farms was heavy and badly drained which made the work for the horses very hard. He obviously had a great love and regard for his horses, indeed all animals, and he included many references to horses and ponies in his poetry.

At the same time as the invention of the collar and the new type of plough, a new and improved draught horse appeared. Until then the native type of horse employed on farms in Scotland was a rather inferior sort of animal. When the Duke of Hamilton imported six black Flanders stallions in the mid-18th century, they were bred with the best of the draught mares that could be found. This was the start of the wonderful breed that became known as the Clydesdale.

By 1830 the combination of new technology and the Clydesdale had led to the demise of the ox as the farm work animal. The new unit comprised two horses, one plough and one man, and was far more efficient than the old plough teams. The timing of this was fortunate, as the Napoleonic Wars were soon to necessitate a vast increase in agricultural output.

By 1850 the Horsemen's Society in some parts of the country had become almost like a trade union and no farmer could work his fields without a horseman who was a member of the Society. It should not be thought, however, that this was like a modern trade union. It was every man for himself when it came to negotiation over wages, and if the ploughman was dissatisfied with his conditions of work, the only sanction he had was to leave at the next term time. But a farmer knew that if he employed a horse whisperer, he could safely leave horses to his care and need not enquire too much into how they were worked. He was happy if the animals looked well and the work was done to his or his grieve's satisfaction.

The advantage for youths of becoming members of the Secret Society was that once they had joined they were regarded as men and the farmer had to pay them a man's wage.

After you were admitted to the Secret Society of Horsemen you were told the 'Word', sometimes known as the 'Grippin Word'. In fact, the Word and the Grip were separate, as the Grip was a special handshake between members. The Word was said to be a magic word which gave the Horsemen control and absolute mastery over horses. It was also said to be the cause of the high illegitimacy rate in north-east Scotland. If a young unmarried woman became pregnant, her explanation that the father was a ploughman was received with understanding. The poor lass could not be expected to be able to resist the power of the Word! It was certainly a great excuse. Many a young ploughman was advised by his elders not to 'try his hand' with the lassies until initiated into the Society. As a member he would be sure to be successful with his courting – he would certainly be more confident.

The Word was not 'magic' as was suggested to outsiders, but as a member of the Society it gave you access to the 'Knowledge' by which you could control horses. Controlling the horse was, in fact, mostly done by smell. The horse has a very profound sense of smell and the Horsemen took advantage of this in many different ways. They mostly used herbs, smells and chemicals. These varied from area to area depending on local availability, but there is a remarkable similarity between many of them, whether in Buchan or Norfolk.

The Knowledge has been passed down the centuries, no doubt refined and altered with changing conditions. Ideas may have been slow to spread long ago, but once ingrained in a culture, they remained firmly in place long after their origins were forgotten. The origins of the Knowledge have mostly been lost, but the following story, still current among members, explains how the first horses were caught and trained to the harness:

> The first horse was caught on a sandy desert on the plains of Arabia. It was a mare that was caught. She was called Bell because she had a bell [white star resembling a bell] on her forehead. It was Juble Cain who caught her. He watched where she went to drink and he made a missie [rope] of camel hair, which he had gathered off the bushes, letting it sail down the water and she sucked it into her mouth. He tried to get her into a shed, but she would not go so he tried to back her in and she left some dubg [dung] at the door. He scattered it over the shed and she jolled it in. The way they got the horse [stallion] was simple. There was a cat's hole in the shed and when the mare came horsing [in season], the horse came and put his head in the hole. When he pushed, a lintel fell on his back, so they knew he could draw and carry.
>
> The first brechem [collar] was made of rashies [rushes]. The first hems [haims – the metal work attached around the collar] were a pair of smith's [farrier's] tongs. The way they knew a horse could stand horse shoes, he stepped on a piece of wood and a nail that had been in it went into his foot and they saw it never harmed him. They made roots of whins [gorse or furze] their first shoes they drove the nails.

The Secret Society of Horsemen, from its beginnings in the north-east of Scotland, soon spread over most of the country, especially down the east coast to the Lothians and into the Borders. It then spread south into England to Norfolk, Suffolk and Cambridgeshire. A few people insist, however, that many of the secrets of the horse whisperers did not spread from Scotland, but were already part of the folk lore of East Anglia before the Society began in Scotland.

With the Scots' tendency towards economic migration, groups of Horsemen were formed by Society members in Canada, the United States and Australia and New Zealand. But by the 1950s, due to farm mechanisation, the Society of Horsemen had almost died out. Small groups have survived, notably in Orkney where, I have been told, members are still initiated into the old secrets; and those societies which appear to have been incorporated into Masonic lodges still flourish.

* * *

These, then, are the origins of the horse whisperers. Although their methods of training and control were very different to those employed by modern whisperers, one thing they have in common is their regard and love for horses. Their philosophy is that you must be kind to horses and treat them with respect. Ancient and not so ancient methods of breaking horses were cruel – even barbaric. 'Breaking' a horse, says it all, and Monty Roberts, the pioneer of modern horse whispering technique, will not use the word. An old ploughman from Angus commented to me, 'Breaking a horse is no good. What is the good of a broken horse?'

CHAPTER TWO

The Horsemen

THE PLOUGHMEN OF THE north-east and east of Scotland, where the Society of Horsemen had its roots and was strongest, were hard men, inured to the cold and difficult working conditions.

They were often small in stature and wiry. They would shave (many had moustaches but few proper beards) if they were going for a drink on a Saturday night or, much less likely, church on Sunday. Their clothing was typical of the time. Early photographs and contemporary records reveal that they wore heavy waistcoats, corduroy trousers and flat caps at a jaunty angle. The caps were often worn on the side of the head and were adjusted from time to time as a secret means of recognising other Society members. On their feet they wore heavy hobnailed boots (called 'tacketie baets') which were repaired regularly and would last for years. Their trousers would be tied under the knee with 'nicky tams' – buckled leather straps. They smoked dirty pipes and often chewed tobacco into the bargain.

They were pretty uncouth, coarse in both tongue and habit. They could be insolent to employers, and if they were, it probably meant they were ready to move at the next term time. Often with a ready wit that was usually disrespectful towards their masters and betters, they were normally polite to strangers but not given to overt signs of affection or emotion. (The 'stiff upper lip' long associated with the English gentry had nothing on a Scottish ploughman!) They might be awkward and difficult but on the whole were utterly honest and took tremendous pride in the quality of their work and thus gave their employers – the farmers – excellent value for money. The individual was judged by his peers on the straightness of his furrow with the plough and the appearance of his horses. Everything else took second place.

Horse whisperers had small regard for organised religion (which in the north-east was the Protestant Church of Scotland) although their secret ceremonies were quasi-religious. 'Respectable' people viewed this as scandalous. The Church had an enormous influence, not to say a moral stranglehold, over the rural population. The ministers of the Church, Calvinist bigots to a man, thundered each Sunday from the pulpit against the sins of adultery and fornication which did nothing to reduce the high rate of illegitimacy, despite 'sinners' (and Robert Burns was numbered among them) having to appear in their local church on three consecutive Sundays to accept public reproof for the sin of fornication. The ploughmen of the Secret Society paid little heed to ministers of religion. If a ploughman happened to get a girl pregnant, he almost always married her, as he was assured at least that the marriage was going to produce children, which were an economic necessity. Children would supplement the family income from an early age by working on the farm.

The common unit of settlement in Scotland, especially in the farming communities where arable farming was predominant, was the 'ferm-toun'. This was a cluster of buildings with houses centred on the farm. The size of a farm was determined by how many pairs of horses would be required to plough and cultivate the land. By the early 1800s a simple reckoning was that on an average arable farm one man and two horses could work about 50 acres of land. A twelve-pair farm was not uncommon. On poorer land where the farms were often much smaller, one or two pairs of horses was the likeliest power unit, with a spare horse known as the 'orra beast' used for odd jobs or to supply occasional extra power. Three horses were usually required to pull the binder (in England three horses was a common unit).

Farming communities in East Anglia were usually based around villages and not centred so much on the farms. The farm workers would live in and around the village with its pub and church and manor house. By and large, village life was more civilised and less isolating for the workers than life on the ferm-toun.

The lowest rung on the farming ladder where hierarchy was all-important and each man knew his place was occupied by the boy just out of school. The term 'orra loon', which comes from the north-east, usually applied to the new boy. It means the spare man. The boy was given work around the farm, usually in the byres, feeding the cattle and mucking out the beasts. He began to learn the Horseman's job by carting home turnips for the cattle or carting out dung from the cattle sheds, using the orra beast. To say his status was low is no understatement. He was the last to be served supper if he ate in the kitchen and he would always be last in the queue, even to wash his face. Little wonder he longed to have his own pair of horses to work and to be called a 'halflin', but first he had to prove his worth. The word haflin is very old and is probably a corruption of the term 'half-hind'. In the 17th-century ferm-touns a 'whole hind' had to supply an assistant – usually his wife – as part of the employment conditions. A hind was a farm servant who was usually a Horseman. In parts of Angus the haflin was also known as 'the little man' which was no indication of stature since 'little' meant 'second'. A haflin was responsible for a pair of horses, and depending on the size of the farm and the number of pairs of horses, would be known as the second or third Horseman according to seniority.

Single men lived in 'bothies' which were known also as 'chaumers' in Banff and Buchan, although it was said the distinction between them was that in a bothy the men would prepare and eat their own food, whereas if they lived in a chaumer they would eat in the farm kitchen. Life in the bothy or chaumer was hard and rough. They were often cold, damp, dreadful places and were usually situated adjacent to or above the stable. While this might be very convenient from the work point of view, it did little for living conditions. Warmth might radiate from the horses' stalls but so too did smells and rats and mice.

A travelling salesman wrote an account of bothy life at the time. He said:

> A bothy was often a low apartment without partition or ceiling, often occupying the space from the gable end of one building to the gable of another. The overall plan of the bothy, within, was a row of undressed deal-beds along each side. There was a fireplace at each gable end but these fires had no chimneys, only narrow slits in the walls to allow smoke to find an outlet. The roof leaked in dozens of different places and along the ridges of the roof the sky might be seen from one end of the apart-

ment to the other. The men in the bothy learned to tell the time when they awoke during the night by observing the stars, which were visible through the openings of the roof. It was, in truth, comfortless habitation for human creatures in a wet and gusty winter's night. The inmates were as rugged as their dwelling was rude.

Of course not all bothies were like the one quoted. The bothy which I remember at the farm at home had a ceiling and was a one-room structure with an open fireplace and chimney against the gable wall and two iron double beds with straw mattresses. Only two men lived in that bothy and they took their meals in the back kitchen at the farm. This however was in the late 1930s; conditions were much harder 100 years before. The haflins as single men usually slept two to a bed. It was warmer that way and they would sleep in their semmits (vests) and 'long john' underwear without any thoughts of impropriety. The beds had straw mattresses which were often ridden with vermin of one sort or another. In some farms the kitchen maid would clean the bothy and make the beds while the men were out of the way at work. Most of the time the bothy was a male-only environment with no need for curtains as the windows would be filthy and covered in cobwebs. Most bothies had an open fire with a 'swee' – a metal or wooden device for swinging a pot or the kettle over the fire. The swee could also be used to lower or lift the pot depending on the amount of heat required.

Furniture in the bothy was very basic. Not everybody had a seat on which to sit, and many just sat on the bed or used sacks filled with chaff if nothing else was available. Each man would have a chest of sorts (known as a 'kist') to keep his personal possessions such as his best clothes for Sunday and, if he was musical as many were, his fiddle or melodeon or hurdy gurdy. This last was a musical stringed instrument, like a primitive violin, whose strings are sounded by the turning of a wheel and was often called 'Auld Nick's (the Devil's) Birlin Boxie'.

The diet was very basic. It was based on oatmeal with which the bothy men made themselves porridge, or 'brose' as the porridge was often called. They ate it from a wooden 'caup' (bowl) using horn spoons, sitting round the fire rather that at a table. Milk and potatoes would be given to them, sometimes for nothing if the farmer had a kindly disposition, and if not, as part of their wages.

Married men or cottars were often better off as they lived in tied cottages separate from the steading (farm buildings) with their wives and children. They were allowed to cultivate a small area of land at the back of the house which was called a kail yard where they would grow vegetables to supplement their diet. Part of their wages was often paid in kind with oatmeal, potatoes and milk. Wives would usually be expected to work on the farm especially at harvest time, and they often had to work even if they were nursing very small children. The older children would bring the infants to the field or steading to be suckled.

Given the conditions of mean and bitter poverty, it is little wonder that men and women would be old and wrinkled before their time and crippled with arthritis.

They worked six days a week, not Sundays, but the Horseman was expected to feed, groom and muck out his horse on a

Sunday morning. The rest of Sunday was free, as the 'toun keeper' was left in charge of the stable. Every man was expected to take his turn as toun keeper. In 1903 the *Fife Herald and Journal* published a rhyme which says it all:

Six days shalt thou labour and do all
That you are able,
On the Sabbath-day wash the horses' legs
And tiddy up the stable.

The working day during the winter months began between three and four in the morning when the men would get up work in the barn until daybreak flailing corn. This was the primitive way to thresh corn before the threshing mill was invented. They would then feed their own individual pair of horses, groom them and muck out the stable before they had their breakfast. After they had eaten they would walk or ride their horses out to the fields to plough the land.

All through the winter months, as long as the ground was not covered with frost or snow or sodden with rain, the work went on, first on the stubble fields after the harvest and then the 'ley' (pasture land). If the weather allowed, men and beasts worked until supper-time without a break, apart, that is, from answering the calls of nature or stopping to fill their pipe at the end of the field. It was a long day, but it must be remembered that in the north of Scotland in the depth of winter the daylight hours, when outside work could be done, were very short.

If the weather was too bad to work outside, more flailing was done in the barn and there was always the horse harness to clean. Before supper could be taken the horses had to be fed and attended to and settled for the night. The men not surprisingly were ready for bed by nine o'clock.

In the summer months things would be a bit easier but the hours were longer due to the longer daylight. The working day was from five in the morning to seven in the evening with two hours off in the middle of the day to give the horses a break and allow them to feed. Experiments proved that the most efficient way to work Clydesdales was two five-hour periods or yokings (i.e. harness work). As conditions of employment improved, six to eleven in the morning and then one to six in the afternoon gradually became the rule. The ploughman's formal commitment to the farmer became a ten-hour day with additional labour open to negotiation such as at harvest, hay and turnip time. The one thing a farmer would never ask a ploughman to do was work with cattle as that would always be refused.

The men, especially single men, worked from one hiring fair to another. They paid their bills at Whitsunday and Martinmas when they themselves were paid. In a large ferm-toun the process of finding whether you would be wanted for the next term could be brutal. The grieve or foreman would come into the stable in the morning, and before he gave out the work for the day he would move up the stable talking in turn to each man he wanted to keep on but pointedly missing out the man (or men) he did not want to re-employ. According to the custom of the time the ploughman understood he was not being 'speired to bide'. There would be no harsh words, and come the day of the feeing market which was held in the local town he would be looking for a new job.

The reason for dispensing with someone was not always that the man's work was not up to scratch. It might be his moral character, he may have displeased his master in some way, or been too ready with his opinion, or his caustic wit in a bothy song may have given offence. Just as often the man himself wanted to move on, possibly to better himself by becoming head horseman at another farm or to get away from a hard task-master or his sharp-tongued wife! Just a desire to work a better pair of horses would be enough reason to make a man take another job.

Before a ploughman left a farm he would try and ensure he got a character reference. Here is a typical one written by a John Wilson, Panbridge Farm near Carnoustie, Angus, at the November term in 1889:

> This is to certify that William Blythe has been in my ser-
> vice as a plowman for seven years, and a more steady,
> sober, able-bodied man is rarely to be found, and I have
> the greatest pleasure in giving him the highest recom-
> mendation to whomsoever may employ him.

Not surprisingly William Blythe treasured this testimonial. He died in 1948 at the age of 92.

Most testimonials were more basic and did not strain the credulity or the grieve's grammar too much, but would smooth the way from one farm to the next.

At a hiring fair men stood around waiting to be approached by prospective employers. When approached, the talk was of money and conditions, and after hard bargaining a deal was struck. The farmer or grieve would shake hands with the ploughman and they would then retire to the nearest inn to seal the bargain with a dram.

When a worker moved to a new farm, especially when a family was involved in the move, one or two carts were sent to carry the family and all their possessions to their new house. The poorest would have very little in the way of furniture and personal possessions, but as the 18th century gave way to the 19th, the cottars would have owned cooking utensils, crockery, tables, chairs, kists, beds and bedding. At term time carts would be crossing and passing each other all over the countryside as families and men moved house and employment.

It would be wrong to think that it was all work and misery for the working man and his family. The men in their bothies made their own entertainment, singing bothy ballads, often with scurrilous words which might well be aimed at bad masters and which never got into print. Music was supplied by the fiddle, melodeon, mouth organ and hurdy-gurdy. Some bothy ballads became very well known, such as *Nicky Tams*. Others have long since slipped into obscurity and will probably never be sung again, such as one man's verse on entering a new ferm-toun and seeing his new pair of horses for the first time:

I gaed to the stable
My pairie for to view;
And, fegs they were a dandy pair,
A chestnut and a blue.

Farm workers hardly ever wrote down their verses, except

perhaps on the back of the barn door, and they were mostly to ridicule the boss: 'If you are going to fee boys, don't fee for Annie Fraser. She has a tongue that would clip cloots.'

The following simple verse was found written in pencil, faded and almost lost, on the barn wall at a farm near Biggar:

The wind whistled in the square
As ploo'man Jock led in his pair
The winter's nie
The fields are bare
And ploo'man Jock gie [very] scant of hair.

Men would play for village dances and would travel some distance, especially once bicycles became commonplace. This was usually done without thought of payment and just for the pleasure of getting away for a time from the drudgery of the job. My own father and his ploo'man Jake formed a small band in the 1920s and performed all around the area with a fiddle and a melodeon.

For many men, especially in the 18th and 19th centuries, the only relief from work was to get drunk at the weekend, often getting back very late and perhaps just in time to saddle the horses in the morning. Some would just fall asleep in the stable if they couldn't get up the stairs to the chaumer.

By the late 18th century, ploughing matches had begun to be popular with both farmers and horsemen. These were instigated by agricultural societies and encouraged by 'lairds' (large land owners) and some of the bigger tenant farmers. They soon became country-wide events and were usually held annually in different districts.

A variation of the ploughing match was a custom which developed whereby incoming tenants to a farm would be given a day's 'darg' [work] by other farmers and ploughmen in the form of a ploughing match. This was to enable new tenants to catch up with necessary work that might have been neglected or not done since the previous tenant left. My own great-grandfather Peter Lyon was given just such a welcome in 1892 on his new farm, when 29 ploughmen came for a ploughing match and managed in a day to catch up with all the ploughing which had not been done during the winter months. As with all such matches, judges were appointed and prizes awarded and traditional hospitality was dispensed to all participants by the grateful farmer and his wife.

Prizes were awarded for the best work. Ploughmen were judged by how neat and straight they could plough a furrow. Prizes were also given for the best turned-out pair of horses and (very often) the handsomest ploughman. Blacksmiths would make special match-winning ploughs, while preparation and burnishing of the harness and horse brass would begin weeks ahead of a special event.

Ploughing matches were great social occasions and the champion ploughman was, for that day at least, a king among his peers.

* * *

This, then, was the farming society in which the Secret Society of Horsemen flourished. The Society has been described as a working-class Hellfire Club. It provided a basis of solidarity among the men and a source of companionship and fun. It also had a less attractive side. It gave a hard time to young and vulnerable initiates and could make life very unpleasant for any ploughman who was unwilling to join and 'shak han's wi' the Devil' – not that many refused the invitation, as it was a world that almost every country boy longed to enter.

John C Milne's poem *Nae Nowt for Me* describes the feelings of the young boy who wants nothing else in life but the chance to work the land behind his perfectly matched pair of Clydesdales:

> Nae nowt for me;
> For aince I leave the Memsie skweel,
> I'll be a strappin foreman cheil',
> And drive a bonny weel-matched pair,
> Big fite horses wi' silken hair,
> And milk-fite mains ahingin doon
> Fae their smooth curved necks like a bridal goon,
> And fine lang tails te swipe the glegs [horse flies]
> Fae their snaw-fite flanks and clean straucht legs.
>
> I'll buy a dandy brush and kame
> To groom them weel at lowsin-time
> I'll rub them doon wi' a cloot that's saft,
> And feed them on bruised-corn fae the laft,
> Swaddish neeps and bran and hay,
> Linseed cake and winlins o' strae;
> And baith my beauties will lie and sleep
> On fresh clean beddin twa feet deep.

CHAPTER THREE

The Oath

First I got on for bailie loon,
Syn I got on for third,
And syn of course I had to get,
The Horseman's grippin' Word.
A loaf of breid to be ma' piece,
A bottle for drinkin' drams,
Ye couldna get thru' the caffhoose door
Without yer Nicky Tams.

THIS TRADITIONAL SCOTTISH VERSE captures neatly the essence of the Society of Horsemen and its rites of initiation. The details of the initiation ceremony in Scotland varied from district to district depending often on the whim of the Horseman in charge of the proceedings.

Admittance to the Society was by invitation only. The young man – a 'loon' or haflin – when he turned 18 (16 in some districts) would receive either in the post, or more likely hand-delivered to his pillow, an envelope with a single horse hair. This was an invitation to join the Society, which he dared not refuse, as he knew he would not be able to stay on as a ploughman without becoming a member. At the very least, should he refuse, all initiated Horsemen would make his life most uncomfortable. But most young lads were only too keen to join as they knew they would henceforth be treated as fully-fledged ploughmen and would command an adult ploughman's wage. Not only that, as a member you would also know the Word which would give you power over horses, and over that cheeky kitchen maid who gave you illicit jam 'pieces' [sandwiches] and then ran off. There would be no more running away when you had the Word!

The ceremony would be carried out around Martinmas, which is in early November. It usually took place in a bothy or chaumer although in the early days it would often be held in a remote barn. In more modern times the ceremony has even taken place in a hotel room. Wherever it was to take place, the ceremony was known as 'going through the caff-house door'. This meant 'chaff house' and may reveal a connection with the Secret Society of Millers.

The weather would be turning cold, often with a frost. The ceremony would take place at midnight, perhaps at another farm so that the lad would have to travel there along with his sponsors (originally four other ploughmen but latterly two), and they would meet up with others on the same mission.

The young boys would be clutching a loaf of bread, a candle and, most important of all, a jug or bottle of whisky, all shivering a bit with cold – or was it fear? The whisky would have cost each individual a lot of money considering how little they earned but it was a price the boys were willing to pay.

The new lads were blind-folded and grasped tightly by the arms before they got to the meeting place. The ceremony was very carefully stage-managed for maximum effect. At the door of the bothy or barn, the oldest ploughman would give three measured knocks and would then scrape the door with a horse-shoe before whinnying like a horse. Before admittance was granted, the conductors or sponsors had to give correct answers to questions which were given from within. In some districts the boys themselves had to answer questions. There are many different versions of these questions and answers and I am going to give two sets which are least like each other.

The older and more impressive version was used mostly in the Aberdeen and Buchan areas:

> 'Wha telt ye to come?' was the first question, to which the correct reply was 'The Devil.'
> 'Which wey did ye come?'
> 'By the hooks and crooks of the road.'
> 'By which licht did ye come?'
> 'By the stars and licht o' the moon.'
> 'How high is your stable door?'
> 'As high as tak the collar and haims.'
> 'Where were you made a Horsemen?'
> 'In a Horseman's hall where the sun never shone, the wind never blew, a cock never crew and the feet of a maiden never trod.'

The following, more modern, version, at least judging by the language, was used mostly in the Strathmore area:

> 'Who is there?' was the first question, to which the correct reply was 'A brother.'
> 'A brother of what?'
> 'Horsemanship.'
> 'What with?'

'A blind man.'

(Then, addressed to the candidate,) 'Did you come of your own free will and accord?'

'Yes.'

'What do you want?'

'Information – more especially to get than to give.'

'How did you come here tonight?'

'I saw the light.'

'What colour was the light?'

'Blue.'

'Why blue and not red?'

'Because red is danger and blue is heart's true.'

'Where did you come from?'

'The East.'

'Why from the East?'

'Because all wise men came from the East and fools from the West.'

(Referring to the candidate.) 'Is he above the age of eighteen?'

'Yes.'

'And below the age of forty-five?'

'Yes.'

'Then come in.'

At this, the door would swing open and the candidates (still blind-folded) and their sponsors would enter the building. If the building had any windows, these would have been blacked out to ensure any outsiders could not observe the secret rituals that were about to take place.

Once inside, the boys, still held firmly, were stripped to the waist or, in some cases, stripped totally naked. Depending on the gathered company this would often occasion much bawdy comment and banter and even some physical horseplay with sexual overtones. This would very much depend on the character of the senior Horseman present, who was in charge of the ceremony.

A contemporary account written in the dialect of the time gives a good insight into how the boys were prepared for what was to come:

Bi i licht o ful hairst meen, wull the chiel tirred tae the weist, clorted wi dubbin, mere's collar owre i heid, an nickytams stappit wi strey, an ae hood-wink tae hap i een. (Sicken a manner wull a annintees be prepared fur traivlin tae i Lan o i Siven Labors.)

The rough translation is:

By the light of a full harvest moon, the lad is stripped to the waist, covered with dubbin [old fashioned polish for harness and boots], a mare's collar placed over his head and his nicky tams stuffed with straw while his eyes are still covered by a hood. In this way is the initiate prepared for travel to the land of the Seven Labours [Ages] of Man.

It was a rude introduction to the Society they were about to join. What came next was worse. The initiates were first asked their names, ages and who had brought them. They were also asked if anyone had sent them or if they had come of their own free will and accord. When they confirmed that they had, they were made to kneel in front of a make-shift altar (usually a bag of corn or oats) on which were placed, like sacrificial elements, the whisky, bread and candle. The 'minister' or master of ceremonies stood behind the altar ready to administer the Oath. For some ceremonies the young men would already have been coached in what to say but mostly they repeated the words of the Oath.

The Oath varied from place to place but the basic elements were the same whether it was taken in Scotland, England, Canada or the Southern States of America. A ploughman from the North East wrote down one version in 1908 when he lived in London. He probably wouldn't have dared had he still lived in Buchan. I have at least six versions of this Oath including two taken directly from Horsemen's notebooks. Most are very similar to the Buchan version:

I of my own free will and accord do hereby solemnly vow and swear before God and all these witnesses that I will always hele [old English *helan* meaning to hide or conceal], conceal and never reveal any part of this secret of true horsemanship, which is to be revealed to me at this time. Furthermore, I solemnly vow and swear that I will neither write it nor indite, cut it nor carve it on wood or stone nor yet on anything moveable or immovable under the canopy of heaven, nor yet so much as wave a finger in the air to none but a horseman.

Furthermore I vow and swear that I will never give it nor see it given to a tradesman of any kind except to a blacksmith or a veterinary surgeon or a horse-soldier.

Furthermore I will never give it or see it given to a farmer or a farmer's son unless he be working his own or his father's horses.

Furthermore I will never give it or see it given to a fool nor a madman nor to my father nor mother, sister nor brother nor to any womankind. Furthermore, I will never give it or see it given to anyone after sunset on Saturday night nor before sunrise on Monday morning. Furthermore, I will neither abuse nor bad use any man's horses with it and if I see a brother do so I will tell him of his fault. Furthermore, I will never advise anyone to get it nor disadvise anyone from getting it but leave everyone to his own free will and accord.

Furthermore, I will never give it or see it given to any one under the age of sixteen [eighteen in most other oaths] nor above the age of forty-five. Furthermore I will never give it or see it given unless there be three or more lawful sworn brethren present after finding to be so by trying and examining them.

Furthermore I will never give it or see it given for less than the sum of £1 sterling [this also varied between oaths] or the value thereof. Furthermore I will never refuse to attend a meeting if warned within three days except in the case of riding fire or going for the doctor, and if I fail to keep these promises may my flesh be torn to pieces with a wild horse and my heart cut through with a horseman's knife and my bones buried on the seashore where the tide ebbs and flows every twenty-four hours so that there may be no remembrance of me amongst lawful brethren so help me God to keep these promises. Amen.

The point of the last piece of the Oath was the belief that if someone suffers a violent death, his body should be buried under running water to try and ensure that his ghost would not walk and trouble the perpetrators of the deed.

The Strathmore version of the Buchan Oath is even longer and more involved and in some detail quite different. It shows how the Oath had grown and become even more specific and refined over many years. It has been included because it is so different from the original version:

> The oath I require of you at this time is a very solemn one before God and man and these witnesses:
>
> That I will always hide, conceal and never reveal to father or mother, sister or brother, wife or winch [wench] or the baby that sits on my knee, any of the secrets or vows of Horsemanship that may be revealed to me this day or any day hereafter. I further vow and swear that I will not give it or see it given on the Lord's day or within 24 hours of it nor on a term night, nor on a market day, nor on a fast day. I further vow and swear that I will attend all brotherly meetings, calls, signs and summonses within a distance of 5 miles if I get 24 hours notice, except in 5 cases, being myself in sickness, or sickness in my family, or going for a doctor, or a house on fire, or attending my master's business.
>
> I further vow and swear that I will not give any information of what I see a brother doing to his horses

unless I can give sufficient proof that he is doing it against the principal rules of horsemanship.

I further vow and swear that I will not give it or see it given to a fool, nor to a liar, nor to a madman, nor to a revealer of secrets, nor to anyone intoxicated with drink nor to anyone I would suspect would bad use horses with it.

I further vow and swear that I will bad use no man's horses with it, nor see them bad used without telling them they are so doing.

I further vow and swear that I will not give it or see it given to any man under 18 years nor to a man over 45 nor to a woman at all.

I further vow and swear that I will not give it to a farmer, nor to a farmer's son unless they are as distant as ourselves and are working horses, nor to a grieve that does not work horses, unless a blacksmith or a horse shoer and to no veterinary surgeon whatsoever.

I further vow and swear that I will neither write it, date it, cut it or carve it, print it or paint it nor engrave it on sand, snow, clay nor iron, paper nor parchment nor anything moveable nor unmoveable under the canopy of heaven, nor wave the least part of it in the air with my finger so as any unlearned person might know what it is.

Now these are the commandments, so if you think they are too hard a bondage on you to bear, you are welcome to your money and go your own way. Please say which you will do.

Now if you break any of these commandments, may I stand before a meeting of Horsemen, met for that purpose, there to confess to them that I have broken the oath that I most solemnly took upon myself before God and man, punished by them as I deserve and my right arm may be cut off at the shoulder, and my innards torn out by two wild horses, then my body to be taken to the sands of the seashore and hung up there until the wild birds eat the flesh from my bones, and it may be a solemn warning to others and show them that I have been a deceiver of both God and man, and made myself a fit companion for the Devil and his angels. May God help me to keep my (Horsemen's) secrets. I've performed my vows. Amen.

This particular Oath is the longest I have found and also seems to be the most recent judging by the use of more modern language. It is even more specific and horrific in tone than the older version which was bad enough. It does say the Oath should not be given to any one who is the worse for drink – presumably conveniently ignoring the aftermath of the ceremony. It also precluded veterinary surgeons from joining the Society, which tends to suggest that in some areas vets were seen as a threat to the Society. Perhaps it was thought that vets would see through the mystique surrounding the Society and exploit the knowledge for their own ends. The ban on vets does not seem to apply now, as when I first started my research into the Horsemen's Society, a whisperer who is still active in the Society in the Orkney Isles offered to make me a member.

The purpose of the Oath was to scare the wits out of the young men taking their vows who would mostly be very innocent and easily impressed. Any young initiate would have been very fearful of the consequences of breaking his vows, which was exactly the intention of the ceremony.

After the Oath was taken, the young men in turn were asked in very gentle and persuasive tones if they would like to write down the Oath 'in order not to forget it'.

If any lad was stupid enough to attempt to do so, he was whacked across the knuckles with a chain or belt and ejected from the meeting. He had of course almost immediately broken the most important vow – secrecy! He would never again be invited to be a member and he knew he could no longer work with horses and would have to leave his job and the farm.

With the last hurdle out of the way, those who were left, being now members, would have their blindfolds removed and clothing restored and be invited to partake of the whisky and bread that they themselves had brought to the ceremony. After they were suitably inebriated they would be asked to shake hands with the 'auld chiel' [Devil]. To the accompaniment of rattling chains on the floor, the boys would be escorted to an even darker part of the building. There they would see in the shadows a figure dressed as the Devil (he would be shaggy and horned and sitting on a stook of corn) who would extend a cloven foot to shake. Sometimes the new member had to put his hand through a hole into the adjoining chaff house. He would then shake hands with the cloven-footed Devil. The hoof was usually the foot of a dead calf or lamb or it just might be a forked stick covered with skin. In some cases the foot was smeared in phosphorous to make it glow in the dark or was heated to add to the sense of terror!

After this the most senior Horseman present would whisper the Word to each new member in turn and more whisky and bread were passed around until all the new members had collapsed in stupefied heaps. The final act of the evening was the last toast:

Here's to the horse with four white feet,
The chestnut main and tail,
A star on his face and a spot on his breist,
And his master's name was Cain!

With that the 'new ploughmen' would be helped home to their beds.

Come the morning – a few short hours later – the grieve and the farmer would be aware they had a new Horseman in their midst who had to be paid a Horseman's wage whether they liked it or not.

CHAPTER FOUR

The Word

MOST OF THE YOUNG MEN initiated into the Horsemen's Society would have woken next morning with a severe headache and feeling distinctly unwell. If they remembered much about the previous evening's proceedings, it would probably have seemed like a bad dream as they stumbled down the chaumer stairs to attend to the horses. Kindly fellow ploughmen would probably have hinted at what lay in store at the induction meeting, but the average young ploughman was very naîve and impressionable. The aim of the induction ceremony was to frighten all new brothers who were taking their solemn vows into total secrecy, and there is little doubt it succeeded every time. The aspirant Horsemen had been told, possibly from when they were little boys, that they needed to know the Horseman's Word before they could properly work horses and be ploughmen.

The night had been full of shocks, terrifying at times, but the biggest surprise of the many surprises at the ceremony was that there was more than one Word. The big disappointment was the discovery that the Word had no magic powers at all! To become a member of the Secret Society and know the Word allowed the young men to be taught the secrets of how to control horses which to outsiders would often seem like magic. It wasn't magic at all, but it was clever, and would still work today! The principal Word was a short phrase, but there were many secret Words, most of which were used as tests when meeting strangers in order to check whether or not they were fellow Horsemen.

To survive in this type of closed society the young initiates had to learn very quickly the secrets, rituals and legends which had evolved over the centuries if they were to be accepted as full members and to be able to recognise other members from different parts of the country and fully participate in the group activities. Probably the very next day, when time allowed, the senior Horseman who had been in charge of the previous evening's ceremony would take the new member to one side and have a quiet talk.

Here is a rough translation of an account of what was said to one young man the day after his initiation. It was supplied by Kenung (the pen name of Ken Davidson):

No doubt my wee hard man, you will have thought I was gey hard with you the other night and so I was. You went through the Grand Initiation Ceremony just like all the other lads who went before you as representatives of the Twelve Labours of Hercules and the Seven Deadly Sins. He [Hercules] was the man I represented last night and no doubt you will never have a sorer or rougher road even although you will live another 49 years until you are 70 years old – if the Lord spares you that long.

Peter, if you are ever rough to any poor dim creature be it cattle or horse the way it was done to you last night, may the Almighty hand you over to Auld Nick himself.

In case you have forgotten the Grip let me show you again. Remember it is just like holding the plough and your mare's name is Peg and you yoke a pair of Asses when together.

He went on to remind the new 'brother', as the young Horseman was now called, of the many new names that he had heard at the ceremony and what they meant. All the initiated Horsemen had second names mostly taken from Greek mythology. Those whom he had known before as Jock or Tam or Willy were also known as Gabriel, Selene and Perseus.

Gabriel from the bible was the Angel from the Lord or Son of God, to the Horsemen the name represented the Saviour or Good Soul or summer. Selene represented the Moon, the Night and the West. Perseus (son of Zeus) was Gallant, Brave and Heroic. Other names were Apollo who cared for Beasts [cattle] and Crops as well being the Greek God of reason, intelligence, music, prophecy and the sun! Lucifer was the Devil, or Auld Nick or Winter. Parnassus, a mountain near Delphi in Greece, meant Big, Strong and Enduring. Helios represented the Sun, Bright Light, Day Time and the East. Hercules or Heracles, the Greek name for Hercules, was in Greek mythology the son of Zeus. He performed many deeds and won immortality among the Gods of Olympus. During his labours, Heracles set up the Pillars of Wisdom at the Atlantic entrance to the Mediterranean. The Rock of Gibraltar is identified as Calpe, and across the Straits is Abyla. Abyla was the Antient brother, Yer Lang Awa [long time away], as well as representing Africa, the Dark Continent and Eternity. Calpe was Youth, Most Thoughts and the Deadly Sins.

The senior Horseman then explained that the main recognition words were Pegasus (the winged horse), Calpe and Albyla. These words were never to be spoken outwith a meeting place but the Horseman gave an example of how they were to be used when meeting a stranger:

Two ploughmen who are complete strangers have just met at a horse fair.

1st Ploughman: 'I yoke a mare by the name of Peg.'

2nd Ploughman: 'I just yoke a pair of asses.'

2nd Ploughman: 'Will you stand me a dram?'

1st Ploughman: 'Are you for whisky or caul pee [beer].'

1st Ploughman: 'Antient Brother.' He then extends both hands with his thumbs up as if holding a plough.

2nd Ploughman: 'Your Long Away.' He grasps the others hands with both thumbs down.

Whereupon, having recognised each other as true Horsemen of the Secret Society, and having shaken hands in the special secret Grip, they could then spend the rest of a convivial day in the nearest inn.

There was a lot to learn, it was very confusing, and more was to come at the next meeting!

According to one tale, a few nights later, when only members of the Society were present in the bothy, more secrets were revealed. A new ploughman had arrived who said he was a brother in the Society. He had to be tested before he could be trusted. Once again the senior Horseman (Hercules) took a leading role.

First came the explanation of how Horsemanship began:

How did we get Horsemanship? Three men had to cross a ford with their carts, which they had an ox pulling, and a woman wanted to get across also. She asked the first one for a lift and he refused her so did the second. Juble Cain was third so he took her, seeing as he was so kind she asked him if he would have Horsemanship or Womanship and he said he would take half of each. They were just in the middle of the ford when she was finished with the half of Horsemanship and the cart was overturned and the woman was drowned, so the half of Horsemanship and all Womanship went down the burn. If we had all Horsemanship we could make horses speak.

A question and answer session then began with the man to be tested surrounded by all the others:

'Are you a man?'
'Yes.'
'Who made you a man?'
'God made man and man made me and the Devil had no hand in it.'
'How do you know you are a man?'
'It was revealed to me that was never revealed to boy or woman and I have been tried and retried and I am willing to be tried by you.'
'Where was you made a man?'

'In the Horseman's Hall or any other place fit for the occasion.'

'Where is the Horseman's Hall?

'In yonder three cornered field, where the foot of a woman never trod.'

'Where is the keys of keys of the Horseman's Hall kept?'

'We got the Hall and the keys were not needed.'

'What was the Hall floored with?'

'Nothing but the feet of good Horsemen.'

'What was it furnished with?'

'Loaves and bottles of whisky.'

'What was it roofed with?'

'The blue canopy of heaven.'

'How many horses do you work?"

'Two but both go as one.'

'Your horse wants a shoe.'

'It will be a lang time before it wears to the knee.'

'Your horse's shoe is slack.'

'The smith's no dead yet.'

'Your horse is blind of one eye.'

'He will see as far ower the brae as you will see through it.'

'Which is the right end of your whip?'

'Any end in time of need.'

'How do you hang up your bridle?'

'By the bits.'

'How many poles does it take to feer a field?'

'Seven.'

'What are they?'

'The three poles, the two horses, the plough and the man.'

'Where do you tie your horse's garters?"

'From the point of the shoulder to the sole of the foot.'

'What is the length of your whip?'

'Seven by nine, and by three, one.'

'What are the principal things about a horse?'

'Action, Attraction and Attention.'

'What are the three principal things about a Horseman?'

'Patience, Perseverance and a good Temper.'

'How many links are there in a Horseman's chain?'

'Seven.'

'What are they?'

'The man, the whip, the horse, the plough, time, patience and perseverance.'

'How could you get a mare in foal and not cover her with a horse?'

'Cover her with a cuddy [donkey].'

'Where was the Horseman's Word first revealed?'

'In the middle of water.'

'Who first revealed the Horseman's Word?'

'A woman.'

'How high is your stable door?'

'As high as no cow will kick.'

'What is the hairiest side of your horse?'

'The side the mane lies to.'

'How many sides has a horse got?'

'Eleven.'

'What are they?'

'Inside, outside, aftside, nearest, backside, foreside, plainside, roughside, upside, downside and hairierside.'

'Where was you made a man?'

'Between the brechem and the hems – a damned tight fit.'

'Wha the divel made you a man?'

'God made man and man made me and the divel had no say in it.'

'Wha was as daft to make you a man?'

'An older and wiser man than myself.'

'How are you three getting on?'

'We all go as one.'

'How did you leave yon twa the nicht?'

'Their heads to the hake [hay rack] and their tails to the wa'. I gie'd them a clap and ca'd awa'.'

'You're a queer ald fish – wha's your faither?'

'An older and wiser man than myself, and wiser than a fool.'

'What is it a mare has and a horse disnae and all other beast and body has?'

'Paps.' [mammary glands or teats]

'How many nails does your whip hang on?'

'Whiles one and whiles five.'

'What is better for your horse than corn?'

'The sweat of your own body'

'Whether bolans was rat tailed or docket?'

'It was neither, it had a tail like a cow.'

'Your horse is a cripple.'

'If you had as many nails in your foot you would be a cripple too.'

'What is the length of your lines?'

'Frae hand to mou'.'

'Where did you leave your plough tonight?'

'Below the moon on top of a stone at the end of a well ploughed rig.'

'What way did you leave your swingle-trees tonight?'

'In the letter A.'

'Where was you made a man?'

'Down in yon valley where the cock never crew and where they wouldna keep an impudent bugger like you.'

'Your horse is blind in one eye.'

'He shall see as far through a whinstone as you'll see up a dog's arse.'

'Your horse is hollow backed.'

'When the saddle is on he is complete.'

'Did you ever count the hairs in your horse's tail?'

'Yes.'

'How much were there?'

'25, 27, 29 and a' the rest.'

This account of the testing of a brother member is very detailed and has to the best of my knowledge never before been published. Clearly by the time the newcomer had come through all these questions he was getting a bit exasperated. He had also probably had a bit too much to drink judging by how his language deteriorated towards the end of the questions but he had surely said enough to satisfy his inquisitors. From his answers he clearly knew much about the secret induction ceremony and the significance of odd numbers in his replies. Most important of all he knew the key phrase, The Word(s) that all Horsemen had to know. Twice in the answers he had said 'as one'. Clearly this man was a Brother of the Society.

The Horseman's Word was and is 'Both as One'; in the Doric it would sound like 'Baith As Yin'. Sometimes this was abbreviated to 'One' or, in many circumstances, the letters were reversed to further confuse and became 'Eno'. The phrase signalled the total empathy between man and horse and again has its origin in Greek mythology, the Centaur – half man and half horse. I have been told this Word by more than one source but most significantly by an active member in Orkney. This is the same person who offered to make me a member and clearly hinted in his correspondence with me that 'One' and 'Both as One' were the Words. He signed off his letters with the phrase, and underlined 'One', when he quite deliberately used the word out of context in the letter.

Although I am as sure as a non-Horseman can be that I am correct in this, I have been told by another correspondent from Aberdeen that the Word was 'Bican'. This was said in two syllables 'Bi' and 'Can' with the emphasis on the 'Bi'. The origin of the Word was apparently from Ancient Persia and the purpose of the Word was to calm the horse down. This Word was used out loud to a horse when it was being difficult or when it was being reversed into the shafts. This in itself is enough to exclude it from being the real Word as this was never spoken audibly and never ever when non-Horsemen were present as was the case when 'Bican' was said.

Of course the secret was not the Word itself. The real secret was the knowledge which they successfully concealed from all outsiders. Non-members were told – if they were told anything – that it was the Word which gave the horsemen power over horses – and women. Many young girls who fell for the charms of a young ploughman were happy to perpetuate the myth that they were powerless to resist.

The practical lessons of horse craft that the new Horsemen were to learn, which took up to five years, started the very next morning after the induction. When the new member, befuddled with drink, had been helped to his bed by the senior ploughmen, he was unaware of the oatcake seasoned with oils of origanum, rosemary, fennel and powdered pad from a foal's mouth which was placed in his right arm pit. This combination of aromatic spices, which were used in the oatcake, was mentioned by Pliny, the Roman historian, who said it was irresistible to horses and women.

When the young lad staggered out of bed at five the next morning probably still feeling dizzy and sick and having had, if he was lucky, just a couple of hours' sleep, the oatcake was retrieved. It now had his smell intermingled with the spices and was given to him with instructions.

After the horses had been fed, watered and harnessed, they were led out into the yard. There they stood with the men waiting for the farmer to give his orders for the day. The foreman would tell the farmer that the orra loon was now a Horseman and would be working a pair of horses.

The new Horseman was told by the foreman to take charge of his pair. As he approached them, the leading horse would lay back his ears and back away. It was not having anything to do with this new man! The spicy, sweaty oatcake in his hand, and remember-ing his instructions, the lad surreptitiously broke it so that no one, especially the farmer, could see what he was doing. He then held it under the horse's nose and whispered the Word. The smell of the spices cleared the smell of the man who had previously been in charge of the pair and replaced it with the sweaty smell of the new handler. The horse's ears went forward and he gave no more trouble and was led away to start the day's work.

It looked like magic to any onlookers not privy to the secrets of the Society, but it was just clever use of one of the horse's main senses – smell. By harnessing this sense of smell and keeping this knowledge secret, the Secret Society of Horsemen were able to attain their undisputed position as master horsemen.

As for the new Horseman, despite his hangover, he felt on top of the world. He was now accepted as a man among men – a childhood ambition fulfilled to be a ploughman in charge of a pair of working horses. Never again would he be asked or expected to work with cattle. He knew that his studies under the master Horseman would go on for years as he was taught bit by bit more secrets in a manner very similar to Freemasonry. He would have to be able to recite the Bible backwards three times in three years but that didn't matter. He was to be told the Four Rules of Horsemanship: To Make Him Stand; To Make Him Lie; To Make Him Hip; To Make Him Hie. It was magic to an outsider but he knew better. It was simply the Ancient Art of Horsemanship.

CHAPTER FIVE

How Did They Do That?

FOR A HORSE TO EXIST in the wild, it needed keen eyesight and a powerful sense of smell. Only the fittest with these faculties survived, and in this way the horse developed into the animal we know today, with eyesight which can be as effective in daylight as in dark conditions. The equine eye has the largest ball of all the land mammals and its retina magnifies objects 50% more than the human eye. The Horsemen understood how important eyesight is to the animal and they employed blindfolds and blinkers to help calm nervous horses. But more importantly, they also knew how vital smell is.

The horse's highly developed sense of smell evolved as part of its very necessary equipment to avoid predators. Flaring its large nostrils when necessary, it could smell a predator miles away with the wind in the right direction! This was very important to the grazing animal and enabled it to remain alert even when grazing with the eyes facing downwards. This hyper-acute sense of smell survived domestication, and modern horses can smell just as acutely as their ancient ancestors.

Vets have known for many years that smell is very important in equine reproduction. Urine and, to a lesser extent, horse dung carry chemicals which the stallion detects when the mare is coming into season. He will sniff the air with a characteristic pose of nose wrinkling and lip curling upward. This is known as the Flehman sign, and most horses can be induced into a

Flehman gesture with various different smells which may differ from animal to animal.

A horse greets a stranger, whether another horse or a man, by snorting with the nostrils flared. It does this in order to smell the stranger. If the stranger is a man and he exhales his own mouth odour, this will often have a calming effect on a nervous horse.

I have been aware since my early years in veterinary practice that horses' sense of smell is very perceptive. Horses are good at recognising the vet just as soon as he arrives in the yard. I say 'he' advisedly, not to be sexist but to demonstrate that most if not all horses can tell a female vet from a male. Many horses prefer to be looked at and treated by a female vet, especially after they have had a series of injections from a male vet. They never forget!

They can be deceived, however. On a few occasions I have looked at an animal which in normal circumstances would shy away in fright when I arrived. Just fresh from a shower and wearing non-veterinary clothing, I was not recognised visually and did not encounter the usual hostile or frightened response. On other occasions I have attended usually mild, well-mannered horses after looking at pigs. Horses do not like pigs or pig smells, and even the best natured can be restless when close to a man wielding a syringe and needle and smelling of pig.

When I first started to research the original horse whisperers, I was to a certain extent aware that smell was somehow used in the control of horses. I thought that it was used in a negative way in that the animal would associate a particular smell with a bad reaction such as being beaten, and as a consequence would obey a handler through fear. I was surprised and delighted to find that the opposite was the case, and control by using different smells was done with kindness and compassion for the animal.

After he had taken his vows of secrecy, a new member of the Secret Society of Horsemen was taught the innermost secrets of the Society. These would enable him to make a horse stop dead in its tracks or, just as impressive, make an animal come to him from the middle of a field without saying a word or lifting a finger.

The term for freezing an animal into immobility in Scotland was 'reist' [arrest], while in East Anglia 'jading' or 'hexing' a horse was mostly used. When a Horseman 'stopped' a horse, whether he was a Scottish ploughman or an English farm worker, it would not move again until someone 'in the know' released it from the spell. If the Horseman appeared to whisper in the horse's ear when it was induced to move again, this only reinforced the superstitious impression that magic was being invoked – which was entirely the intention.

To stop a horse, the old horse whisperers would place some sort of powder or substance close to the animal's head or to where it was going to pass. The smell, not obvious to human nostrils, would be obnoxious to the horse. Many substances could be used and they were usually organic and mostly connected with blood which a horse dislikes intensely.

A common formula used in East Anglia was dried stoat and rabbit's liver held together by a substance called 'Devils Blood', a red resin which came, I understand, from a palm tree. This recipe was said to have come from a Suffolk ploughman who had watched a stoat kill a rabbit while working his horses in a field. The stoat had first paralysed the animal with fear before it moved in for the kill. The ploughman's horses would not pass the spot where the kill had just occurred, and on investigation the man found both the stoat and rabbit dead. After he had moved the dead bodies the horses were 'released from the spell' and moved on without further fuss.

Different horsemen in different areas had their own hexing or stopping potions. Although most of these were derived in some way from blood or blood products, other substances would work (soot was used frequently) and often just as well. There were many local variations and recipes. A common trick in Scotland to stop a horse from walking out of the stable was to smear the doorposts with pig muck. This smell would not be apparent to any onlooker, but the horse would be aware of it and would not come out through the door. It was also possible to make the animal resist having its collar placed over its head by using the same trick. A mole-skin could be employed in a similar way and was occasionally used malevolently by smearing it on a manger to stop an animal from eating.

Ploughmen used all sorts of means to demonstrate their ability to stop a horse. A tale told frequently is how they would stick a fork in a dung heap and hitch a horse to the fork. The animal would strain every muscle but could not pull the fork out – at least that was what an onlooker saw! The Horseman at the head of the beast may have looked as if he was giving every encouragement to the animal to pull, but so long as he had an obnoxious smell concealed in his hand, which only the horse was aware of, the animal would not move from the spot.

Urine was another method. Stallion men would keep the stallion's urine in a bottle until the smell became very powerful. It would then be used in small drops either on the stallion's bridle or on a mare to make sure the stallion would not go near that particular mare.

The practice of reisting or jading a horse is very old and not just confined to the Secret Society of Horsemen. Nor was it confined to men only. I was told of an old widow who lived in the early part of the last century who clearly had some jading knowledge. She lived near Stamford in Lincolnshire and was called a witch, since if any one upset her she could stop their horse at her door and it would not move until after payment of a 'small consideration'. She would then lift the spell and the horse could continue its journey. I suppose her husband had told her the secret and she used it very much to her advantage. It was almost as good as a pension!

There are many tales of tricks played on horse owners and ploughmen not privy to the secrets of the horse whisperers. A ploughman who did not know his place in the hierarchy on the farm or was cheeky to the head Horseman would fairly soon find his pair of horses almost impossible to handle – even to get out of their stall. He would quickly learn, if he wanted a more peaceful existence, to be more respectful towards his elders and betters. If he did, his animals would soon be restored to their former compliant mode of behaviour.

Many jading stories are based around visits to the pub. It was common in East Anglia for Horsemen to stop at the local if they were passing by with their team. It could be the Devil's own job to get the men out before too much drink was consumed, to the detriment of their work the next day. The horses knew the way home, and many a well-oiled ploughman would climb into the cart, fall asleep and not wake up until his horse walked into the stable yard.

A farmer who had a particular problem with one of his men asked the local policeman to look out for this man, and if he ever saw his horses standing outside a pub, to get him out of it and send him home. The policeman took his job seriously and the next time he saw the farmer's horses outside The Fox, he went inside and told the man to get back to the farm. The man said he would, but only when he was ready. The policeman was not best pleased with this response and threatened to take the horses back to the farm himself. The response was not encouraging. 'Right,' said the ploughman, 'if that's your attitude I'll stop here until closing time.'

The policeman went out and tried to lead the horses back to the farm but they would not budge an inch. He eventually gave up and went back into The Fox to admit he could not shift them. 'No more you will,' was the response, 'they'll go when I'm ready.' The ploughman quietly took his time to finish his drink and then took the horses home without any trouble.

Another Horseman who was confined to his bed through illness was concerned that the second Horseman was overworking his horses. He got members of his family to each fetch an ingredient of a jading substance so that no one member knew the full recipe. The mixture was then daubed on the field gateposts, stopping the horses from passing through. This practice was occasionally also used to stop equipment such as ploughs being used without permission of the head Horseman.

Having bewitched (or so it seemed) an animal into refusing to move, how did a horse whisperer undo the spell? For those with the knowledge it was simplicity itself.

The obnoxious smell had to be neutralised in some way, usually with another smell which the horse found acceptable. A common solution was a mixture of milk and vinegar which the

Horseman would rub into his hand. He would then rub his hand over the horse's muzzle and into its nostrils. While he was doing this he would talk quietly to the animal and give the appearance to any onlooker that he was whispering the Word.

A man who was not a member of the Society of Horsemen knew enough to overcome the 'spell' when his horses were reisted from walking through a stable door. All he did was wash the doorposts with water and the problem was resolved without difficulty. A more modern method of overcoming a jading chemical which is very effective is to rub an empty salt and vinegar crisp packet over the horse's muzzle.

It was not always necessary to use a neutralising smell to get a jaded horse to move. Blowing into its nostrils, especially if the breath was heavily saturated with tobacco smoke which the animal would probably recognise, could be highly effective both for neutralising whatever the jading substance was and calming a difficult animal. Charles Dickens, in *David Copperfield*, describes how Uriah Heep was observed blowing into a pony's nostrils and immediately covering them with his hand, 'as if he were putting some spell on them'.

Experienced Horsemen knew that sharply twisting the animal's head away from the source of the jading substance and then forcibly backing it away from the affected area would work. However, as this did not appear in any way magical and was something any experienced horse handler could do, it was only done in private and never in front of a non-Secret Society audience.

The opposite of being able to stop a horse was the ability the whisperers had to draw or attract horses to themselves even from the middle of a field. Most horse owners will know the frustration of trying to catch a reluctant animal. Horse whisperers never had this problem.

To the uninitiated it would seem like magic when some scruffy little man with his cap at the side of his head would stand at the gate of a field and all the horses would trot up to him. He had not said a word, he didn't make any secret signs with his hands, nor had he resorted to bribery with a bucket of feed. The whisperer knew it was enough to stand upwind of the animals and allow them to get a sniff of the 'drawing' or 'calling' oils which he used. All the oils used were very aromatic. Most common were oil of origanum, rosemary, cinnamon and fennel. It was sufficient on a warm day to smear some drops on clothing or a sweaty forehead. Onlookers only saw the man who smelled of stale sweat and the stable but the horses knew differently and would gather around him very quickly.

The following advice on 'drawing' oils came from an old Horseman's notebook which went on to give further instructions for catching difficult animals such as wild colts and vicious beasts in a large field or common. The method was similar to that used after the initiation ceremony to enable a new member to handle a horse.

The instructions stated you had to bake a scented cake using oatmeal flour (about half a pound) and treacle. These were baked together slowly, and when the cake was ready it had to be sweated under your armpit to take on your smell. It was then scented with cinnamon, rosemary, fennel and virgin oil. You were then advised to stand with this upwind of any stroppy nag and the animal would soon come to you. Once the horse had tasted the cake, you would have a job getting rid of it and it would always be attracted to you. If you did not have time to bake the cake, gingerbread treated in like manner would do just as good a job.

Many natural and sometimes unnatural compounds were used as drawing or attracting substances. The chestnut that grows on the inside of a horse's leg (often known as the caster) was used as a base for a drawing powder. The pad that foals have in their mouths when they are born (usually known as the milt) was also greatly prized and commonly used by Horsemen. In both cases the material was allowed to dry out or was baked, and then ground into fine powder. For the powder to be effective, it would have to be impregnated with aromatic oils such as those already described, although some said that if the oils were too potent this would reduce the natural effect of the caster or milt. Oil of rhodium was often recommended to be blended with the powders as it did not overpower the natural scent of the drawing powder. The powders were extended by combining them with oat flour and they were then bound with oil. It was said that with these powders horse taming was easy.

The recipe that follows uses the chestnut on the horse's leg:

> Procure some horse caster and grate it fine. Also get some oil of rhodaim and oil of summin (presumably cummin was meant) and keep them in separate and tight bottles. Approach the horse on the windward side and rub summin on his nose and give a little castor on a piece of loaf sugar or potato. Put eight drops of oil of rhodaim in a tumbler between your fingers and thumb to prevent it getting out. As soon as you open his mouth empty on his tongue and he will be your pet.

The Caithness Agricultural Society was the source of two remedies for taming horses. The first was quite specific:

Tincture of Opium: 10 drops

Oil of Aniseed: 15 drops

Oil of Thyme: 10 drops

Oil of Cinnamon: 10 drops

Oil of Rosemary: 10 drops

Oil of Nutmeg: 10 drops

'Mix all these ingredients with 2 drams of orris powder and apply a little to the palm of the hand and rub it across the horse's nose. If you do all this to the letter, the animal will obey you completely.

Apart from the use of aromatic oils on the animal's sense of smell, the tincture of opium would have a natural soporific or calming effect on the horse's brain.

The second remedy is very strange and involves a plant called a marsh orchid. This plant has a root with two bulbs which are known as 'bull's cods' or 'dog's doddles'. The trick was to break the bulb into two and put both bulbs in a bucket of pure spring water. The bulb or ball that sinks is 'hate' and maddens a horse, and the bulb that floats is 'love' and quietens the animal. It sounds like a piece of superstitious nonsense, but the bulb that floated to the surface would be treated with drawing oils which would make it attractive to the animal. Presumably it did not matter which bulb rose to the surface, for so long as it was 'cured' with the right blend of oils and perhaps sweated in the arm pit, it would prove highly effective in attracting a reluctant horse.

Individual Horsemen became renowned for their ability to tame and calm animals. One of the most famous horse whisperers was an Irishman called Sullivan who was well known for taming the wildest, most vicious, obstinate horses that no one else could handle. His most famous exploit was when he tamed a stallion called King Pippin at the Curragh. This animal had almost killed a man in 1804 by picking him up and shaking him like a rat. It was said the man was only saved from greater injury by the thickness of the clothing on his back. Sullivan was small and a bit too fond of a drink, but he always responded to calls for help. On this occasion he shut himself up with the animal all night, and in the morning the horse followed him out of the stable 'like a well trained dog'. The stallion then won a race at the meeting and, it was said, remained docile and tractable for about three years. Unfortunately, it then reverted to its previous vicious behaviour, killed a man and was shot.

On another occasion, Sullivan, who worked alone and always behind closed doors, tamed a colt that no one could approach with safety. He was shut in the stable with the animal for only half an hour and at the end of that time a signal was given to open the door. When it was opened, Sullivan was found lying on the straw beside the colt, playing with it as if it was a puppy.

Sullivan never divulged his secrets to anyone. It was said he was a charmer and whispered to the animals he was taming. Many who knew him thought he had supernatural powers, and one priest thought that he was in league with the Devil. When the priest met him he would make the sign of the cross and move to the other side of the road. This behaviour annoyed Sullivan considerably and it all came to a head one day when he and the priest met head on. The priest told him he was 'a confederate of the wicked one'. At this Sullivan jaded the priest's horse and would not release it from 'the spell' until the priest agreed to leave Sullivan alone forever. Sullivan died an alcoholic in poverty in 1810, and although his secrets died with him, there is little doubt he knew and used the secret formulas and potions known only to members of the Secret Society of Horsemen.

Another well-known whisperer was a man called Chaplin who worked with Shire horses in Essex in the early part of the 19th century. He answered an advertisement for a man to lead a Shire stallion. Stallion leaders were men employed to lead stallions from farm to farm to cover mares in season. It could be a difficult and sometimes dangerous job as some stallions were very hard to handle in the breeding season.

When Chaplin reached the farm he was told that the animal had killed the last man who had attempted to master it. Chaplin, undaunted, took up the challenge. The farmer warned him that the horse would attack him as soon as he opened the stable door. Chaplin waited until it was dark and then put on a long white shepherd's smock. He opened the door without warning and the horse backed away puzzled by the white apparition. Chaplin, seeing the horse confused, dropped to his hands and knees and crawled into the stable with the animal retreating before him. The door closed behind them and when it reopened Chaplin was in complete control of the stallion. There is little doubt that Chaplin had followed up his surprise tactics by using drawing oils on the animal, which from that time on gave no further trouble.

The men who travelled the 'staigs', as stallions were known in the north-east of Scotland, were legends in their own lifetime. They tended to be loners with unsavoury reputations which were no doubt exaggerated by the job they did, but they were members to a man of the Society of Horsemen. Their control over their animals and their knowledge of medicines and lotions was amazing, and typically they were sought after by the ladies of the many parishes they visited. Paternity suits tended to follow around after them. Perhaps girls were just as attracted to aromatic oils as horses! It was said that kitchen maids were made insatiable by innocently accepting a sticky sweet (touched lightly by a drawing oil or even stallion's saliva) from a travelling man.

Whisperers employed all kinds of methods when first meeting a difficult horse. One Horseman in Norfolk used his cap! He would throw it into the horse's stall. It was no doubt impregnated with aromatic oils which the animal could not resist. The Horseman would say that if the horse welcomed his hat then he too would find no opposition! Another whisperer used a small stick to the same effect. It usually had a split at one end into which he had inserted a plug of wool saturated with a drawing oil mixture. He would throw the stick into a difficult animal's manger. The horse would almost inevitably be drawn by the smell to the food trough and would stand and allow himself to be caught and handled.

Horse dealers used sticks impregnated in the same way when they walked animals back to their yard after buying them at a market. There are many tales of how a dealer would walk home with the new horses following behind him without a rope or halter on them. Again, people thought it was the whisperers' secret Word at work.

Horsemen took great pride in the way they drove horses. After becoming whisperers, many of them after a time would be able to control their pair without the use of reins. They would often walk or ride them to their work in the fields without direct control through the bit and bridle. While ploughing, the reins would be slack, the animals knowing as well as the man what had to be done, but for all that, for one man to control two big animals, which were in many cases as heavy as a ton each, was impressive.

Not all whispering stories are farm-related. A correspondent told me a tale from a time when the cavalry was an integral part of the Territorial Army. Her grandfather came from North Uist and each year travelled to the mainland to do a fortnight's training with the Militia, as the Territorial Army was then known. While they were in camp at Inverness one of the horses went completely out of control and no one could handle the situation. A soldier stepped forward and claimed he could calm the horse. He approached the deranged animal, spoke quietly to it, and to everyone's amazement, the animal stuck its head under the man's arm. It became completely docile and was quietly led away. Grandfather was most impressed and asked the man how it was done.

It was arranged that Grandfather and the soldier should meet at the edge of a wood that night. They walked into the wood and stopped at a spot indicated by the soldier. Grandfather was then asked to shake hands with the person in front of him. As he could see no one he protested that he could not shake hands with an invisible being. He was told that when he repeated certain words, the invisible one would materialise. In fact, he was being asked to renounce God and deliver himself to the Devil. This Grandfather refused to do and the matter ended there. He maintained ever after that what he had observed was black magic, but it was obvious from the story that the soldier was a whisperer and had drawing oils in his armpit which calmed the horse. The soldier would not divulge the secret of whispering without first making Grandfather swear the oath of silence. This he refused to do and remained in ignorance the rest of his life.

Sandy Aitken was a foreman on a farm in the 1920s. He was known to have the 'Horseman's Word' and was kind and careful with all the animals in his care. Every night at about 8 o'clock the six horses in the stable were given a feed of corn. After they finished, he put them to bed – he walked along the stalls and touched every animal on the rump and told them to go to sleep, whereupon they all lay down as directed. It was a quietly impressive scene, which no doubt over a period of time had become a conditioned reflex, but it never failed to amaze the unbiased witness.

Sandy Aitken was typical of his time and type. These were quiet patient men, members of a secret society with an almost mythical understanding and partnership with horses in their care. They had many secrets, but most would agree with one old whisperer's words of encouragement to a new member: 'Be kind to them, laddie, an' they'll do anything for you.' That was the most important non-secret of all.

CHAPTER SIX

Black Magic, Superstition and The Moon Men

THE BELIEFS OF THE SECRET Society of Horsemen had an under-current of superstition which some think originated with the Picts and Anglo-Saxons. The Romans held many of the superstitious beliefs to which horse whisperers subscribed – Pliny, Juvenal and Virgil believed in the power of the foal pad or milt and mentioned its value as a love potion. They probably learned this from the Greeks, as Aristotle mentioned it as a substance which improved the love of the mother for a foal.

The strangest superstitious belief had nothing to do with the foal pad but instead with a frog or toad bone. The secret cere-mony in which the bone featured was known in East Anglia as the 'Waters of the Moon' and the men involved were called 'Toad Men' or 'Moon Men'. Those who took part believed that the Devil was involved in the ritual. It took a great deal of courage to invoke the help of the Devil, but that was what many Horsemen in Norfolk, Cambridgeshire and Suffolk believed they needed to do to empower themselves to handle horses. Most Horsemen in the Secret Society thought that using a frog or toad bone, due to its supposed links with the occult, was the most effective way to control a horse.

Although some of the rituals of the Secret Society came to East Anglia from Scotland, there can be little doubt that the superstition connected with the frog's bone was known among whisperers in England for many centuries before the Scottish horse whisperers became organised into formal groups.

An old Norfolk Horseman described the East Anglian ceremony. The ritual was practised in countries as far apart as Scotland and India. In India, as described by Sudhin H Ghose in *The Flame of the Forest*, the frog was killed, wrapped in a piece of white linen and given religious blessings. It was then put in an anthill at sunset. The ants ate the flesh and left the bones. This process was no doubt faster in India due to the hot climate than in the more temperate East Anglia. Two of the bones were used. The first one, the scapula (shoulder bone), also called the shovel, was used to attract a lover. The other, the ilium from the frog's pelvis, was used to spurn a lover's advances.

Horsemen in East Anglia preferred what they called a walking toad, and some talked of a black frog with a star on its back. This was a natterjack toad, usually found in woodland and recognisable by the ring around its neck. The toad or frog was killed and then put on a white- or blackthorn bush for 24 hours until the carcase had dried out. It was then buried in an anthill or sometimes a dung heap for at least a month, or from one full moon until the next. When removed, only the skeleton was left. This was kept carefully until there was a full moon and it was then taken at night to a stream of running water. In some accounts of the ceremony the Horseman had to go alone and put the skeleton in the running water. It had to be watched very carefully, as a small bone would become detached from the rest of the skeleton and float upstream against the current. This was the 'magic' bone – the one to be saved.

While the bone was separating from the rest of the skeleton strange noises could be heard, sometimes like wind rushing through the trees or a building falling down or even a noise like a traction engine. On no account could you take your eyes off the bone – if you did and looked backwards to find the source of the noise, the power would leave the bone. It was supposed the noises were caused by the Devil at work in the middle of the night. Much more likely the sounds were created by other members of the Secret Society who followed the lone Horseman to ensure that any new member observed the proper ritual and was aware this was a serious, secret business, not to be taken lightly! No doubt the weird noises were magnified by the almost hallucinogenic effect of staring at an object and running water for a length of time.

The bone was described as being forked like the wish-bone of a chicken and was probably the ilium. It has been remarked by many that it was also shaped like the frog in the horse's foot. This is a triangular, horny, elastic pad essential for the wellbeing of the horse's hoof.

When the bone was recovered from the stream, it was dried, and then usually baked, after which it was crushed into a powder and kept in a sealed container. The powder was often mixed in a bottle with some oil such as linseed. In this way you could put some on your finger or on a handkerchief and wipe it on the nose, chin or muzzle of the horse to give you absolute control over it.

Many Horsemen did not powder the bone but used it whole after it was dried. It was wrapped in a special piece of fabric, usually linen, and then always taken with you, as you never knew when it was going to be required. Some Horsemen carried it unwrapped in the armpit in order that it was impregnated with their body odour. To stop a horse they would touch it on the shoulder, and to release it from the jading they would touch it on the rump.

There seems little doubt that most of those Horsemen who took part in the ceremony of the Waters of the Moon believed totally in the supernatural effect of the bone. It was even whispered in Scotland that the bone in some cases was taken from the finger of a dead child but not surprisingly there is no documentary evidence for this. Many men were so badly frightened by the occult ceremony in which they had taken part that it prayed on their minds. There was even a belief in East Anglia that any man involved with the ritual of the frog's bone would either eventually go mad or come to a violent end. Certainly many Horsemen in Cambridgeshire, Norfolk and Suffolk must have felt very isolated, alone and afraid, as they lacked the support and mutual assurance of the Secret Society of Horseman which so sustained Scottish Horsemen.

The fact of having invoked the Devil caused nightmares. One man had a persistent dream that his stallion was coming to his bedside as he slept. He told his wife who was no doubt fed up with having her sleep disturbed. She said that nothing had gone right in the house since 'he had truck with the Devil', and told him to get rid of the bone. He dug a large hole and filled a tin box with milk and vinegar. The bone was put in the box and it was placed in the hole and covered with clay. The Horseman had no more bad dreams but ever after he never got on so well with his horses. No doubt his self-confidence around horses had been buried along with the bone.

Although most Horsemen who had a bone believed it conferred occult powers on them, many knew that the real reason for their powers was that the bone, which could so affect the behaviour of the horse, had been cured or treated with herbs and chemicals and this was the main reason the bone had the effect it did.

There were many different methods for curing the bone, and depending on how it was cured, the material could be used for allurement or to stop an animal. One Suffolk Horseman described his method of curing the bone in order to attract a horse. He wrapped it in brown paper and placed it in the oven after the bread had been removed and the oven was cooling down. When the bone was dried, it was pounded into a powder and mixed with some oat flour and oil to form a small cake and baked again in a cooling oven. When the cake was ready, a few drops of rhodium were added, it was sweated under the armpit and was then ready for use. This particular Horseman used the same method for curing the foal pad.

Others did not bake the powdered bone in a cake but just mixed it with selected herbs and chemicals of their own choosing. With a little oil added and then deposited in small quantities on an old rag or on a finger, it could be used easily in a surreptitious way on a horse's nose or tongue.

Animals, in particular horses (and dogs), are very aware when a person is frightened or tense when handling them. A horse will take advantage immediately of anybody who is apprehensive in any way. A man with a toad's bone in his pocket would be supremely confident in his ability to handle and dominate the animal. The horse would be aware of this confidence, act accordingly and become quietly submissive.

The rite of the Water of the Moon was fairly well known in East Anglia but there is less evidence that it was commonplace in Scotland. New members of the Society in Scotland had to take part in other superstitious rites which arguably were even more frightening than the frog bone ritual. The ordeals were designed to test the new member and find out if he really would blindly follow instructions and place his trust in his fellow Horsemen.

An initiate would be directed at the dead of night and in the pitch dark to an old churchyard close to the meeting place. He had to follow a certain path which led to the church and then walk between the tombstones until he reached the correct stone – say the third on the left from the stone dyke. This had to be done alone, as he was told that at the correct stone if he searched beneath it – the gravestone was usually flat on the ground – he would find a whip which would give him power over any horse he was likely to encounter. As he searched for the whip a hand reached out from the grave and grabbed his. The Horsemen of the Society had positioned a member beneath the stone ready to give the new man the biggest fright of his life. It is not difficult to imagine the terror induced in a young ploughman by such a prank, but the lesson that lay behind the ritual was that no matter what happened, if he trusted his fellow brethren, no harm would come to him. It was in a sense a test of his manhood and strength of character that he could undertake such an ordeal.

Many superstitious beliefs and rituals involved being in a graveyard at midnight when everybody knew that ghosts, ghouls and demons roamed abroad which made the place even more terrifying than at other times. It was a brave man who could uncover a grave and remove a screw from the lid of a coffin while reciting the Lord's Prayer backwards. Such a screw would reist a man or animal from moving if it was screwed into a victim's footprint, again while the Lord's Prayer was recited backwards. This was said to be a favourite method of a Yorkshire witch who stopped a ploughman's team in the middle of a field; but the ploughman was equal to the spell, as he broke it by touching each of his horses with a whip stick from a rowan tree. The witch ran away shouting a curse: 'Damn the lad with the rowan-tree gad.'

The rowan was said to have mystical protective qualities. It was common practice in some districts when horses were turned out overnight during the summer months to protect them from witches by tying a rowan twig or a cross made from rowan to their tails by means of a red thread. If this protection was not provided, it was thought that witches might use the animals for nightly expeditions to Spain and other far-off Mediterranean lands.

Even a stabled animal was not safe from being 'stolen' overnight by witches. Evidence that a horse had been used was to find it sweated up and exhausted in the morning. There are, of course, natural explanations for these phenomena. The horse may have had colic [abdominal pain] which can cause sweating. And if the stables were near a coastline such as in Suffolk, then it was not uncommon for the horses to be 'borrowed' by smugglers in the dark of night to move contraband, in which case the animals would be found next morning tired and sweating. However, the supernatural explanation was useful, especially if the smugglers had bribed one of the Horsemen. Saying that witches had taken the horses for night-time excursions and caused their exhaustion would get the Horseman out of any potential trouble from his boss.

Pieces of rowan were fixed above a stable door to prevent witches' entrance. Holly was occasionally substituted for rowan but tended to be used somewhat differently. Its prickles were used to scratch a horse's flanks for protection against evil spirits. The plant was also thought to protect against nightmares caused by a horse goblin, and twigs of holly were often found hanging in bothies to protect the sleepers.

In medieval times a foal's cowl, which is the piece of placenta that covers the foal's head when it is born, was hung up in the stable as a witch repellent. This was supposed to be especially effective in protecting a young unbroken animal which found difficulty settling. No doubt the remedy appeared to work because the animal gradually got used to its new surroundings, but the improvement in behaviour was attributed to the presence of the afterbirth.

A hag stone, which was most commonly a flint-stone with a hole through the middle, was often used in stables to keep witches at bay. It was mostly suspended over the animal's hindquarters to stop the witch from mounting the horse.

A horseshoe was said to have the same effect as a hag stone in scaring off witches and the Devil, as it was both metal and man-made. The tradition of the horseshoe being repulsive to the Devil goes back to an old legend of St. Dunstan who was a farrier. The Devil, being cloven-hoofed, was said to have asked St. Dunstan to put some shoes on his feet. St. Dunstan first tied up the Devil so that he could not move and then hurt him so badly nailing on the shoes that the Devil vowed never again to enter a building where he saw a horseshoe hanging up.

The tradition of the lucky horseshoe goes back a long time. Pliny the Elder, the Roman historian, recommended a horseshoe to ward off evil spirits and bring good luck. Lord Nelson sailed into battle at Trafalgar with a horseshoe nailed to the mast of *The Victory*. Even now the horseshoe is regarded as a good luck token and is often carried by brides and still incorporated in house signs, and to find one unexpectedly is thought to be an omen of especially good luck.

Brasses, used to this day to decorate horse harness, began as symbols of good fortune and although their supernatural origins have long since been forgotten, they are reminders of a pagan past.

As a veterinary surgeon I am relieved when the warmer weather comes along which allows pregnant mares to foal outside in the fields. Mares have far fewer gynaecological troubles when they have their foals in natural surroundings. Mares foaling indoors may become 'cast' and have difficulty in standing up after giving birth. A stable can be a confined space in which to move around, and when a foal is just finding its feet and is very unsteady, a clumsy mother knocking it into a wall may damage it. Outdoors is also a far cleaner environment than a stable and both mother and offspring are much less liable to post parturient infection. Horsemen instinctively knew these things, but a supernatural twist was put on basic knowledge.

Recorded in Banff in north-east Scotland in 1890 was the fact that mares were not allowed to foal indoors as the youngster would later be an untrustworthy horse. In the event of it being born in a stable, the evil effect would be counteracted by the foal being pushed backwards out of the building. In some cases, the stable door would be taken off its hinges and laid flat in the doorway in order for the foal to be pulled out backwards by the tail. If a mare foaled in a stable, she would often have a small piece of rowan tied to her tail by a red thread to protect the womb from the evil spirit of infection.

* * *

James VI of Scotland and I of England, like many of his subjects, had an irrational fear of witchcraft, black magic and sorcery. With his book *Daemonologie*, he did much to foster and encourage a mania for persecuting ordinary folk who, although by and large having no knowledge of witchcraft, mostly believed in witches and warlocks. During his reign a wave of accusations, trials and executions swept the country. These only really began to die away in the 18th century when common sense started to prevail. By 1736 an Act of Parliament finally stopped legal persecution for alleged witchcraft, but Parliament and judges were not the general public and especially not the Presbyterian Church in Scotland. Ministers would rail from the pulpit against witchcraft and those who dabbled in it and deny any person perceived as transgressing in this way the right to receive communion. This was a very powerful weapon, as the accused would become a religious and social outcast.

Ordinary people would take the law into their own hands. Suspected witches were made to swim in the local pond after having their hands and feet tied together. If they sank, they were innocent; if they floated the case was proved, for the water 'refused' them.

Some people volunteered to be tested rather than endure the suspicions of neighbours. In 1792 an old woman in Stanning-field wanted to be tested to allay suspicion among her neighbours. She was thrown in the village duck pond and was dragged out, half drowned. A magistrate reproved the woman's husband for allowing such stupidity, but his excuse was that his wife had threatened to kill herself if she was not allowed to disprove her neighbours' fears.

In 1825 a man called Isacc Stebbings from Suffolk was accused of bewitching a farmer's wife. He suggested he be put to the water test and went to the village green with four men and the parish constable. On two occasions he floated and a third trial was arranged, but an enlightened village vicar stopped proceedings.

Horse whisperers and the Society of Horsemen may well have been obsessed with secrecy partly because they were terrified that they might be accused of sorcery. Of course, there were always people who simply asked for trouble. Many a ploughman boasted he could make a horse turn a rig [furrow] without using the reins to guide it. Not many said they could make a plough work a rig without man or horse! The young ploughman who did offended the wizard Laird of Skene by his boasting. The wizard reisted him so that he could not move:

An' there he stood as firm's a rock
For a' that they culd dae
Till Skene cam bye an' spake a word
Which set the ploughman free.

It probably taught the young man a lesson he never forgot.

It was never too young to learn. Thomas Lindsay was only twelve when he boasted that, for a halfpenny, he could make a horse stand still in the plough by turning himself 'widdershins' [anticlockwise]. His fate is not disclosed.

Many of the practices of the Society of Horsemen could have been viewed as Devil worship and witchcraft by an ignorant general public when they were in fact no such thing. But not even the most experienced Horseman could resist some superstitious beliefs, and we can hardly scoff at this when in the 21st century there are still people who will not walk under a ladder and will touch wood – just in case! However I doubt many in this day and age would take a newly acquired horse to the nearest running stream, as did the Horsemen of old, and there 'light off with the horse's hinder feet in the water, and tak up a handful of sand out of the water, and three several tymes straik the horse from his ferret to his shoulders, and then to his taile and all the evil spirits should not have power to wrong his horse in knee or thigh'.

CHAPTER SEVEN

Recipes, Cures and Strange Concoctions

THE FIRST RECORDED EVIDENCE for the treatment of animals was found on a fragment of papyrus excavated in Egypt which was dated to around 1900 BC. On the fragment were recorded symptoms of disease, treatments and prognosis. Treatments included bleedings, application of cold water and the use of vegetable oil. This is no 'magic' or superstition. Bleeding animals has only in recent times been discarded from rational treatments. Using cold water to reduce swellings is a very useful remedy, as anyone who has used a cold hose on a swollen equine limb will testify. Vegetable oil is given frequently for the treatment of constipation and is an important and useful laxative.

Knowledge of animal disease and treatments percolated down the ages from the Egyptians to the Babylonians – the second great civilisation of the Middle East – and then to the Canaanites. Around 1500 BC the inhabitants of Canaan wrote down on clay tablets preparations for the treatment of horses. The tablets must have been the very earliest veterinary prescriptions. The drugs which were derived from fruit, flour and herbs were introduced into the nostrils of horses. Because of damage to the clay tablets, it is not clear exactly what type of diseases were being treated, but it appears that these people had a profound knowledge of horses and knew how important smell was to the horse. They were the early predecessors of the original horse whisperers.

Their knowledge was passed on to the Greeks who were skilled in the use of medicine. The Greeks understood that heat, cold, overworking, insufficient work, and feeding immediately after work could be harmful to an animal. This sounds simple and self-evident to a modern mind but it is important to understand that ancient people concerned with husbandry and animals were considering the animals in their care and attempting to understand their animals' needs. Many of the ancient remedies and treatments which the original whisperers used may have originated during ancient times.

The Romans in turn learned a great deal from the Greeks and employed many to look after their horses and oxen which were used as beasts of burden and were so very necessary to keep the Roman army supplied. Pliny considered that the horse was as complicated a subject as man from the medical standpoint and he had learned this from another Roman called Varro who had made a study of Greek culture and veterinary medical practice.

The first recognisable recipes from Roman civilisation bear some resemblance to those used by Horsemen two hundred years ago. Horses were not often shod in the Greco-Roman period, so everyday maintenance of their feet was vital to keep animals mobile, and to this end hooves were coated with products to protect and promote the horn in the foot. A commonly used ointment consisted of: 1.5 kg tar, 0.5 kg wormwood, 9 heads of garlic, 0.5 kg lard, 0.75 litre of old oil, 1 sextarius of vinegar. The ingredients were mixed together and boiled, and when cool applied to the feet. This recipe would have been recognised – perhaps with the exception of the garlic – and used by Horsemen in both Buchan and East Anglia.

Although the Romans often treated their horses with brutality and would not have recognised the concept of being kind and caring towards their animals, there is no doubt that the treatment of horse ailments and illnesses advanced greatly in the Roman era.

When the Roman civilisation ended, history descended into the Dark Ages, and between 500 and 1200 AD there is no written documentation of any treatment or care of horses or any other animal by anyone who might be classed as having specialised veterinary knowledge. This does not mean that horses were not receiving care and attention. As a commodity they were much too valuable to be ignored and discarded when injured or ill, although they could be and were eaten.

The use of black magic and the practice of sorcery appear in an Anglo-Saxon book in which a recipe is given to remedy damage inflicted on a horse by elves and dwarfs. Much Anglo-Saxon superstition had pagan origins, but as Christianity became the main religion, Christian rituals began to appear, as in a recipe which states:

Take a knife whose handle is made of the horn of an ox of tawny colour and which bears three bronze nails. Trace the mark of the cross on the forehead and on each leg and then in silence, pierce the left ear of the animal.

Other recipes were just as ridiculous. One treatment for

constipation was to catch a lively brown trout and make the constipated animal swallow it live. The idea must have been that the trout would swim through the intestines and somehow relieve the obstruction. Perhaps this procedure was partially effective due to the animal being so frightened that there was a cathartic effect on the gut.

Among the well structured groups of Horsemen who belonged to Secret Societies in Scotland, recipes, treatments and cures were shared but kept closely and jealously guarded from outsiders. In England and particularly East Anglia where Horsemen were far less organised in groups, recipes and cures tended to be an individual's secrets and were handed down from father to son in many instances. Keeping a useful remedy secret would ensure that your services would be preferred to those of another man with less knowledge. To share the information might reduce your advantage in the job market when work was scarce.

There were thousands, even hundred of thousands, of recipes and cures in use until the advent of modern medicine and technology made most of them redundant. Many cures were very similar and varied only slightly in content. The Horsemen in East Anglia and north-east Scotland used the same herbs, oils and chemicals to improve the general condition of their horses and to cure them when they were unwell. Remedies were handed down by word of mouth but many were written down in notebooks by individual Horsemen and also in veterinary books of the time. Some remedies can be viewed even today as potentially useful, others as perhaps harmful and even dangerous, and others as just plain daft.

* * *

Horsemen spent much time grooming and giving thought to how their horses' appearance could be improved. Feeding was vital, and every man was responsible for feeding his own animals from the common source of food that the farmer made available. A ploughman would always attempt to procure just a little more for his pair, and give little extras in the form of a swede or turnip or a few carrots or an apple which he knew the horses would enjoy.

Included in this care were remedies to enhance a horse's condition and make his coat gleam. Simple ingredients such as herbs and roots were to be found in the fields and hedgerows. Many of the old Horsemen in East Anglia used bryony roots. These were scraped and moistened and added to the horses' feed. Bryony had to be used with great care, since in any quantity it is poisonous, as any book on British poisonous plants will tell you. However in small quantities it would make a horse's coat shine. Other Horsemen used burdock which they would first dry and then use the roots in a similar manner to bryony. Elecampane, a plant similar to the aster, was in frequent use in some districts. It gave a horse an appetite when it was very tired. Elecampane has a broad velvety leaf and it was the leaf that was used. The herb was in common use in medieval times and was even made into beer. There is a rhyme about it:

I have a little bottle of Elecampane;
Here Jack, take a little of my flip-flop;
Pour it down thy tip-top;
Rise up and fight again.

Most country people are aware that clippings from a yew tree or hedge are deadly poisonous to all livestock including horses, but I found a reference for the use of yew to improve a horse's condition. The Horseman said he would take a double handful from the tree, which had to be from the 'he' yew tree and not the 'she' yew tree, wrap it in brown paper and put it under his mattress for a year. When he took it out, it was dry and crumbled like a fine powder. This he put with 'other stuff' and mixed it in the horse's feed. He said it was sometimes difficult to get the horse to eat it because it was 'rank poison'. He said it would kill a horse within a week if it was not used correctly, but if it was used properly the animal's coat would shine and it would get very fat. But this is an example of a remedy that must not be tried under any circumstances. Even if you know the difference between a 'he' yew and a 'she' yew, it is liable to kill the patient very rapidly.

Chemicals may have been used more by Scottish ploughmen than their English counterparts as the Scottish climate, being colder and wetter than in England, made natural products less easily available. Here is a Buchan recipe which includes chemicals and is for cleaning a horse's coat and making it shine:

1 lb Silver of Antimony
1 lb Sulphur
1/2 lb Nitre
1/2 lb Cream of Tarter
Mix together and give the horse 1 oz three times a week after water.

Other recipes for feeding include the following:

11/2 oz Black Antimony, 2 oz Gentian Powder, 11/2 oz
flores [flowers] of Sulphur and the same of Tinne Greek
[presumably Fenugreek which is a type of clover.

Even simpler is:

1/2 lb Sulphur of Iron, 2 oz Ground Ginger and 3 drams
of Anseed [aniseed].

These recipes all have ingredients that can be seen to have
potential benefits for the horse's digestive tract and hence the
skin and coat. Aniseed and ginger are powerful digestive stimu-
lants, fenugreek is mentioned in many preparations, and flowers
of sulphur have long been used in medical prescriptions.
Antimony, however, is potentially lethal if given in any quantity,
but if used with caution was said to be an excellent medicine.
Its possible lethal effect did not seem to deter the donor of a
recipe from the north-east:

Liver of Antimony, Steel of Antimony, Sulphur, Nitre
and Cream of Tarter all to be mixed together and given
to each horse three times a week after water.

This, he said, was guaranteed to clean a horse's coat (get rid
of dandruff and scurf) and make it gleam and shine.
Another recipe involving Antimony was very specific:

Nitre in powder – 12 oz, Antimony in powder – 8 oz, Flour of Sulphur – 4 oz. These ingredients should be well mixed and divided into 24 equal parts. One part should be given night and morning for 12 successive days. It should be given alternately one day in bran mash and the next in corn damped with water to allow the powder to adhere to it.

The author stated that these powders 'have a wonderful effect in purifying the blood and bringing the horse into condition; and for a stallion I particularly recommend that one series of doses should be given before the covering season and repeated when it is over.' He went on to say that the recipe proved beneficial to animals that were hide-bound, low in condition and not thriving. 'The horse should be stopped from working while taking the powders and should not be exposed to rain or cold, and his drink should be a little warmed if the powders are given in cold weather.' This author is typical in that he gives quite specific instructions and states that if these are carried out to the letter, the medicine is bound to be effective no matter the ailment.

Although many ploughman had their own remedies, some preferred to buy patent medicine from chemists and drug companies who peddled their cures around the countryside. John Rowley, druggist at the Red Cross in The Poultry, London, was one such. He offered all sorts of ingredients such as aniseed at 6d a pound, gentian at 7d, liquorice at 6d, ginger at 34s per cwt and so on. The list was endless, and the goods were sold at his premises or could be ordered by post, or bought from travelling salesmen who would call at farms with the various ingredients.

Three young ploughmen outside the stable door at Kirton Logie, Buchan. The man on the left is Alexander Middler. (by kind permission of GC Middler)

YTHANSIDE FARMERS CLUB PLOUGHING MATCH.

Alexander Middler at the Ythanside Farmer's Ploughing Match, 1908. He was about 18 years old. Note the cart in the background, which was used to transport the plough. Alexander Middler died in 1973.
(by kind permission of GC Middler)

Five pairs of Clydesdales in Angus, late 19th century. Note the new corn-stacks and the stack poles to keep them standing through the winter.

(by kind permission of W Bryce; the man on the far right was his great-uncle)

Ploughing behind a pair of Percheron at a match near Attleborough, Norfolk.
(by kind permission of Mrs Hilda Burrows)

A Percheron standing patiently while the cart is loaded with sugar beet at Banham in Norfolk. (by kind permission of Mrs Hilda Burrows)

Three Shires pulling a rib roller at Bradwell, Great Yarmouth. James Randell was the man behind the roller; his son, George Randell, is holding the horse.
(by kind permission of Mrs Phyllis Harwood)

A Clydesdale horse standing while the stooks of corn are unloaded directly onto the stack. The photograph was taken near Dundee around 1940.
(by kind permission of DA Smith)

Clydesdale horse and cart photographed in 1905 at Kingennie Farm in Angus. This is much like the horse and cart on which the author sat as a small boy.
(by kind permission of DA Smith)

Medicines and ingredients were also sold at horse fairs and sales throughout the country.

Some of the simplest remedies may have been the best and the least harmful. Nettles once they have been cut prove irresistible to most horses and will be eaten with great relish. Horsemen would cut and dry nettles in flower and incorporate them into their horses' feed. Nettles have a high iron content and this may be the reason they do seem to be beneficial.

Another simple, cheap and probably very effective recipe is a method for protecting horses from flies. The remedy was used all over the country, as I have found references to it in notebooks from Aberdeenshire to Norfolk. A recipe from Perthshire states:

> To protect a horse from flies, take two or three handfuls of walnut leaves and pour on three quarts of water. Let them infuse all night and pour the whole next morning into a kettle and let them boil for a quarter of an hour. When cold the mixture is fit for use. Before the horse goes out of the stable, moisten a sponge and let those parts which are irritated be smeared over with the liquor namely between and up on the ears, the neck and the flanks.

It goes on to state that if it is a riding horse, the lady or gentleman who rides out on it will be delighted by the fragrance. There are few remedies listed in this book which I would recommend any horseowners to try, but this may well be one of them. It certainly won't do the animal any harm and might well work.

It is worth mentioning here the Horsemen's methods for changing the colour of a horse's hair and for dappling the hair.

To change the hair on the head of the horse, take a soft woollen cloth, soak it in brine or salt solution. Mark the spot on the forehead with chalk then apply the cloth above mentioned for three nights and this will very shortly bring about the effect desired.

To dapple a horse:

This important secret can only be affected in later spring or early summer and you require to gather the buds of the Ash tree. Give the horse to be operated on one handful to eat each day for a week and the dappling effect will be in a very short time.
To make horse hair grow:

Honey one ounce, camel oil half an ounce, mix well and put it in the place which the hair is wanted to grow.

Stallion handlers, or leaders, were almost always members of the Secret Society of Horsemen. These men were a breed apart. They needed to know all the secrets of their trade which was to handle the stallions that covered the mares. The end result – the foals – was all-important and a stallion that could not or would not serve his full quota of mares in a season (up to 300) was a serious economic loss to his owner.

First of all it was important for the animal to be in good

health. For good health the animal's digestive system had to be in good working order, there had to be no constipation and the horse had to have a healthy appetite. A hand-written recipe from an old notebook gives the following advice:

> To make a horse cover when he is unwilling first give him half a pint of West Indian castor oil to keep his bowls [bowels] clean open a few days before you want him to cover then a few hours before going to cover give him as follows:
>
> 2 tablespoonful of tinteure [tincture] of conthandus [cantharides or Spanish fly] or 2 tablespoons of tinteure of lytic or oil creben or 1/2 oz spirit of nitre or 1/4 oz of juniper and if these fail then you may give him one tablespoon of tinteure euphorbian but this requires great experience.

For a stallion which is slow in covering a mare the same author suggests 1 teaspoon of tinteure of Ringwood in a mash every night and 'if that doesn't work a teaspoon of cantharides in the mash every other night'. He then states that 'he (the horse) will then be ready at any time.'

Most Horsemen knew that Spanish fly was the most important ingredient and did not mess about with others. They got 1/2 oz of Spanish flies and gave one wet in the feed twice a week. The same remedy could also be given to mares to bring them into season. The mare was given 11 drops of essence of Spanish fly, a portion 'that has never been found to be wanting'. Spanish fly was a well-known aphrodisiac not just confined to use in stallions and mares and is a substance (active principal cantharidin) derived from a bright green beetle known as the blister beetle which was dried and then crushed before use.

Most stallion leaders and Horsemen had lots of ways of getting a mare to conceive. Some were bizarre, as one method related by an old Horseman shows. He would stand in front of a barren mare, and as the stallion was 'a-seeding' [ejaculating] he would jab a knife into the mare's nostril. 'Not far,' he explained, 'just about quarter of an inch to let the blood rush out and that would do the trick.' He also said he had tried the same trick with a retriever bitch that could not have pups and it had worked well. He had learned 'the trick' from his father. No doubt as far as the mare was concerned, having a knife jabbed into her nose took her mind off what was happening at the other end and she would be less likely to lash out at the stallion!

Many ploughmen did not want their mares to be put in foal as they would lose the use of them for a time, but if the farmer wanted a foal, they would have to be seen to be co-operating as the horse was not the ploughman's property. However, there were ways round the dilemma for Horsemen with the right sort of knowledge. The medicinal herb saffen or savin, which is related to juniper, was used in some parts of the country as an equine contraceptive. In East Anglia it was known as the three-penny-bit herb as the dose of the leaf of the herb was just enough to cover a silver three-penny piece. Put in the mare's feed daily, it would ensure she would not conceive. Some stallion leaders would not allow their stallions to cover mares on a farm where saffen was seen to be growing, because they knew the herb might have been fed to the mares and it would be a waste of time and the stallion's energy to cover a mare that had been given saffen.

If a mare was not in foal, she would come into season and would be responsive to the stallion. Unfortunately this was not fool-proof, as some mares, even although they were not in foal, did not come back into season. It was said that the best test for pregnancy was to drop a little water in the mare's ear. If she was in foal, she would shake her head, if not, she would shake her whole body. This test apparently worked for two weeks after the mare had been served. It was even possible to tell whether the foetus was male or female by looking at the mare's flank. If the foal was to be a colt, the hair rises up, and if a mare, the hair lies down. And to get to know the colour of the foal, 'get some of the mare's wash, bottle it airtight and keep it for eight months and the colour floats to the top'. Quite how this would work if the foal was destined to be skewbald or pinto is not clear!

As working conditions for men and animals were hard, and long hours in the cold and rain were normal, there were high incidence rates of arthritis, harness chafing, muscle aches and pains and sore backs – and that was only the ploughmen! It is not surprising that there were many ointments and embrocations – for both ploughman and horse. Based mainly on turpentine or sugar of lead, they would impart a warm glow to a sore area. Here is a typical recipe:

To cure a sore back, get a gill of linseed oil, 2 oz of turpentine and 2 oz of spirit of wine, mix well and rub them on.

And a mixture for bruises or green wounds:

Take tincture of myrrh, oil of turpentine, oil of swallows and oil of pike an equal quantity of each. Shake them together in a bottle and dress the wound twice daily.

These mixtures would increase the blood supply to a damaged area and speed up the healing process.

Until quite recently I sold horse 'white oils' in my veterinary practice. This contained turpentine and was sought after by dustbin men and football players as the best remedy for aches and pains.

A mixture for sores and wounds which was popular in the Aberdeen area contained 4 oz resin, 3 oz bees wax, 1/2 lb lard and 6 oz turpentine. The ingredients were dissolved in a pipkin with gentle heat. To them were added 6 oz fine powder of verdigris, stirred with a stick and strained through a coarse cloth. When the mixture was cool it was said to be an extraordinary ointment for a wound, bruised hoofs or broken knees.

Worms have always been recognised as very harmful to the horse. Modern treatments are extremely effective in controlling worms. Old remedies were not, but this did not stop Horsemen trying many different medicines to try and kill internal parasites which they knew could severely debilitate or kill their animals.

Celandine was used in East Anglia to clear a horse with worms. The plant was dried and added to the horse's feed, but it is doubtful whether it did the animals any good at all. More complex was a treatment from the Angus area which states:

Give him a mash for a day or two and then tarterised antimony two drachms, two drachms spirit of turpentine, three ounces linseed oil, this mixed well together in 1/2 lb of feed. Follow in a day or two for a week with sulphate of iron, 1 drachm, 1 drachm powdered gentian, 1 drachm powdered pimento and 2 drachm of powdered ginger mixed with treacle.

This mixture may well have got rid of a few large roundworms but I doubt would have much effect on the others and must have given the animal a nasty dose of diarrhoea.

As well as drastic purges such as castor oil, many Horsemen would use tobacco as an infusion in an attempt to get rid of worms. It is possible that tobacco with its active principal nicotine had some paralysing effect on worms, but it is also highly toxic to the horse and had to be used with great care.

Diarrhoea was a common problem in young horses. Fortunately there were many mixtures which offered fast and effective relief. A common recipe consisted of 1 drachm powdered ginger, 2 drachms gentian, 1/2 drachm opium and 1 oz prepared chalk. This mixture could be given two to three times daily and would work well. Unfortunately, if the cause of the diarrhoea was intestinal parasites or bacterial infection, the affliction would tend to recur when the treatment finished. However, if the cause was poor management or bad feeding, the treatment was often highly effective and the diarrhoea would be cured.

The active ingredient was opium which is most useful in any preparation as it drastically reduces gut motility and stops diarrhoea whatever the cause. When I was newly qualified I prescribed it as tincture, but unfortunately, due to human drug abuse, opium is no longer available for use as a veterinary medicine. It was freely available to the general public from most chemists 150 years ago.

Coughs and colds were very prevalent. The causes were not well recognised, as viral and bacterial infections had yet to be discovered. Many horses were often kept within a common airspace and ventilation in the stable area could be very poor. In addition, the stable atmosphere was inevitably full of dust and fungal spores from the hay. This is now known as a primary cause of what was originally called 'broken wind' and we now recognise as a form of equine asthma. Animals with broken wind would have great difficulty breathing and became unfit for work. Ploughmen had no knowledge of the real causes of respiratory problems apart from cold and damp but they knew that the situation would improve if the animal was turned out into the fresh air.

Of the many different recipes for coughs and colds, lots involved nothing more than smearing treacle or syrup on the tongue to give relief to a niggling cough. Others were more complicated:

> Take 1/2 drachm of powdered aniseed, 2 oz liquorice, 2 oz caraway, 1/4 lb of powdered squills. Mix together with syrup of Buckthorne. Make ten balls and give one every night.

A ball or bolus was a convenient form in which to give medicine to a horse. As many keepers of horses will know, it can be very difficult sometimes to get a horse to take medicine in a feed. Its sense of smell can detect anything out of the ordinary. A bolus is a small compact ball of medication mixed with lard or butter which would sit comfortably in the hand. It was a very skilled job to administer the bolus, as the hand containing the bolus had to be placed in the back of the animal's mouth over the tongue before the medication was released to be swallowed. The risk of having the fingers badly chewed was high and only the most experienced Horseman would attempt the task.

Medicines could also be given as a drench. This was where liquid was poured into the animal's mouth or down the nostril while the head was elevated. This too was a very skilled job as although the fingers were not at risk, the animal was! Getting it wrong could mean the medicine would either be coughed all over the person administering the drench or it could be inhaled into the horse's windpipe and settle in the lungs with disastrous consequences. The animal could develop an inhalation pneumonia which would inevitably prove fatal, or it could even drop dead at the Horseman's feet.

There was a lot for an apprentice horse whisperer to learn. It is not surprising that it would take up to five years of training and teaching from the senior Horsemen before a young man would know most of what he needed to know to work successfully with horses. There was a lot more to it than getting up in the morning and walking behind a plough all day.

Nowadays, what the Horsemen of old had to learn would constitute a degree course at an exalted university. But they learnt everything on the job, and most of them would not have wished it any other way.

CHAPTER EIGHT

Husbandry and Horses

THE PRIDE AND JOY OF a ploughman on a ferm-toun was his pair of horse and he was judged by their condition just as much as by the straightness of the furrow he could plough. Although he did not own them, he would go to any lengths, including pilfering, to procure that little bit extra feed for his animals.

Horses were mostly fed oats (known as corn in Scotland) grown on the farm and stored in the corn loft or barn. The grain was bruised or crushed by the foreman or grieve. He would put up to a ton of grain through the bruising machine at any one time and it was a very dirty, dusty job. It is necessary to bruise grain before feeding as the husk of the oat is very fibrous and relatively indigestible. After it has been bruised it becomes much more nutritious and edible.

It was the grieve's job also to supervise the distribution of feed. Such a valuable commodity had to be in the charge of a responsible man, as the ploughman was always after that bit more. If he was a cottar he might also be tempted to purloin some for his hens which he kept in the vegetable garden next to his cottage. Every ploughman would take about 2 cwt (100 kgs) of bruised oats at one time and place them in his personal corn kist. The grieve would watch to see that the kists were not emptying too rapidly.

In addition to oats, the ploughman would collect a daily supply of bedding straw from the straw shed and carry it in bundles to the stable. (In poorer ferm-touns, oat straw was used as fodder as well as for bedding, and this was especially common in the early part of the 19th century.) The horses were mucked out in the winter at least twice a day and bedded down with clean straw. Each man would attend to his own horses and would have his own 'graip' or fork for the job.

By the latter part of the 19th century most of the farms as a matter of course fed hay since it was more nutritious, although it was more expensive to produce. In many stables there was an opening into the hayloft above each animal's stall, so that all a ploughman had to do at the end of the day was stand on the manger and reach up into the loft for the hay which he had already prepared into a suitably sized bundle.

In *The Book of the Farm* from the second half of the 19th century the feeding regime of the Clydesdale was given:

From the beginning of October to the end of March, hard worked horses in Scotland are fed three times a day. The morning feed in some cases where high feeding is the rule consists of 5-7 lb of bruised oats; the mid-day feed 4-5 lb of bruised oats and 3lbs crushed linseed cake and as many raw swede turnips, well cleaned and given whole as they will eat, oat straw given as fodder... In spring, when horses are doing hard work for ten hours a day, many Scotch farmers give full supplies of hay instead of straw.

The author of the book, Henry Stephens, knew what he was talking about as he had farmed in Angus between 1820 and 1830.

As conditions gradually changed for horse and man over the years it was realised that it was better for the horses if they had two hours off at midday to give them a break and time to have a double feed. By the 1920s a Clydesdale would get about 3 lbs of bruised oats from the ploughman's corn-kist at each feed time. The grain was measured out in a 'coggie' or 'lippie'. Although the horses might be finished work by six o'clock, they would always be checked and given a last feed and drink of water at eight o'clock in the evening.

Unlike most modern stables, water was not laid on to individual stalls, and the animals would drink from a communal water trough which was usually next to the stable door. Pails of water would be taken into the stable for the evening drink, but many Horsemen would just let the animal walk out to the trough unsupervised, as the older horses knew to walk back into the stall when they had finished.

In the summer months the regime was different as horses were usually out at grass from mid-May until the grass had gone in the autumn – October at the latest. But they would still need a feed, especially in the middle of the day if they were in heavy work, and depending on the nutritional quality of the grass.

In 1894 Robert Dempster from Alyth gave his opinion on feeding and general care of the horse. This has stood the test of time and even today sounds very sensible and full of good advice. He states:

The horse in general is very healthy, especially when carefully fed, groomed and cleaned out. A hot bran mash on Saturday evening is very good for them when on hard meat [i.e. oats]. Nitre and sulphur can be added as the occasion requires. Nitre cures slight colds. Give warm aired water to drink in the morning. Feeding should be done regularly. When the animal is away from home too long, they should have meat in due time. When food is to be changed it should be done with care – grass, etc, mixed with something to keep them from taking a bellyful too quick. Along with corn and hay, the following can be given in small quantities:- Oilcake, locus cake, carrots, Swedish turnips, steamed potatoes, barley steamed at least twenty-four hours. Give salt, or have rock salt in the animal's dish. Always groom well. Keep the joints all brushed out. Always keep the animal's bed dry. Be good to the horses, and they will be good to you.

There was often a constant struggle between what the Horsemen wanted for their pair of horse in the way of feed and what the farmer could afford. Many a tight-fisted farmer would be castigated in song for poor treatment of his horses, and it is possible that the most common reason for a man moving from a farm at term time was when he could not bear to see 'his' horses badly fed.

Good feeding was vital for a healthy horse but regular grooming was just as important to make the animal's coat shine and gleam. A good Horseman would groom his pair morning, noon and night with a dandy brush and curry comb for the body and a comb for the mane and the feather of the legs. Before dandy brushes became common-place, a wisp was used.

This was a simple home-made brush made from a twist of hay like a rope but bound together. Apart from appearances' sake, which was particularly important if the horse was going to a ploughing match, it was vital for the health of the horse that all the sweat and mud that had accumulated while working was removed at the end of each day. If grooming wasn't done properly the animal would be vulnerable to skin infections. Skin infection on the legs (now called mud fever) was called grease due to the appearance of the lesions. The same infection on the body is called rain scald. Without proper care and attention from the Horsemen these infections would be very prevalent. Skin infection is still common-place today in working horses with heavily feathered legs and is now known to be caused by a dermatophilus fungal infection which is brought on by dirt, damp and cold. In the better ferm-toun stables in Scotland, as well as being groomed, the horses' legs would be washed down at least once a week with soap and water to try and keep them as clean as possible.

Horses were often partially clipped with hand clippers twice a year – just after harvest when the winter coat was beginning to thicken and again after the New Year. This in modern terms was a trace clip and it ran from halfway up the chest all the way back to the flank. This was not to improve the look of the animal but to stop it sweating heavily when it was working hard.

Most of the time the horse's tail was allowed to grow as nature intended. In hot weather, however, it would be 'plaited up' into a bun like the bun on the back of an elderly spinster's neck. The mane would also be plaited for special occasions such as shows and ploughing matches. When the hair on the tail was clipped off, as it was occasionally, it would be sold to a travelling salesman. Ploughmen were often allowed to keep the sale proceeds as a perk, but the reward was often not financial but another curry comb!

The ideal of horse care is well described in a verse of John Milne's poem, *Nae Nowt for Me*:

I'll buy a dandy brush and kame
Te groom them weel at lowsin-time
I'll rub them doon wi' a cloot that's saft,
And feed them on bruised corn fae the laft,
Swaddish neeps and bran and hay,
Linseed cake and winlins o' strae;
And baith my beauties will lie and sleep
On fresh clean beddin twa feet deep.

This standard may not have been often achieved, but there is no doubt that the vast majority of ploughmen did their very best for their pair of horses according to the knowledge current at that time.

The hub around which ferm-touns in Scotland rotated was the Clydesdale. A pair of Clydesdales formed a wonderful partnership with the man behind the plough. No man would dare or would even want to set foot in the farm kitchen or bothy for his meal before he had fed, groomed and mucked out his horses. There was little sympathy in a ferm-toun for a man who ill-used his Clydesdales. A man was easily replaced – good horses were not.

Clydesdales are easy to handle and good-natured but this

does not mean to say that the occasional animal would not attempt to squeeze a man against the stable stall partition that separated one horse from another. Hooves could fly, and if a heavy horse kicked you, as I know to my cost, it hurt for weeks and might even mean a broken leg. The odd horse would be jittery and might bolt at an unexpected noise. This could be disastrous and end up with the animal and cart in a ditch with limbs and shafts broken.

Clydesdales were called short pithy names such as Bell, Dick, Bess, Jock, Tam, Jean, Clyde (naturally enough), Prince and Sandy to list but a few. They were usually first put to the harness (yoked) at about two years old, were in their prime at about seven years old and ready to retire at fifteen. Some were born on the farm where they worked and others bought from dealers. In the 1870s a good Clydesdale in its prime was worth about £80, which was a considerable investment and about three times the yearly wage of the ferm-toun's head Horseman. By the 1920s and 1930s prices had changed little, but a good beast was worth about £100, which was still twice the yearly wage of a cottared Horseman.

The Clydesdale derives its name from the district in Scotland – Clydesdale (now called Lanarkshire) – through which the River Clyde runs. The main characteristics of the breed (which had originated in the mid-18th century after the 6th Duke of Hamilton imported Flemish stallions and put them to the native work-horse mares) had been determined by the beginning of the 19th century, and its official debut under the name Clydesdale was at the 1826 Glasgow Exhibition. The Clydesdale Society came into existence as the result of a meeting of breeders on the eve of the Glasgow Stallion Show in 1877. When the stud book was opened in 1877, over 1,000 stallions were registered.

The Clydesdale is a quality heavy horse. It is tall. A stallion can measure from 17 to 19 hands (1.7 - 1.9 metres) at the withers and can weigh up to one ton (1,000 kg). The female measures from 16 to 18 hands and weighs 13 to 18 cwts (900 kgs). It was bred and was ideally suited for both farm work and hauling coal, and to this day is still used on farms and in forests all over the world.

The Clydesdale head is fine and alert with a straight profile – no roman nose! The eyes are bright clear and intelligent, the muzzle wide and the nostrils large. The legs are long and clean with plenty of fine silky feathers below the hocks and knees. Cow hocks (turned inward) are common due to the need to breed animals that could turn easily at the end of a furrow. The feet are very large and round (like soup plates!) and shoes can measure more than 22 in (50 cms) from end to end and weigh up to 5 lbs (2 kgs). These shoes have to be reset or the feet re-shod every six weeks. For all the size and bulk of the animal, it is renowned for being very nimble footed and precise with a high-stepping action. The most common colour for the Clydesdale is bay, and black and brown with roan; chestnut and grey are less frequently seen.

The men who owned, bred and worked Clydesdales were very proud of and enthusiastic about the breed. Few of them would argue with the sentiments expressed in the poem *The Clydesdale* (author unknown):

Thudding hoof and flowing hair,
Style and action sweat and fair,
Bone and sinew well-defined,
Movement close fore and hind.

Noble eye, and handsome head,
Bold, intelligent, well bred;
Lovely neck, and shoulder laid,
See how shapely he is made.

Muscle strong, and frame well-knit,
Strength personified and fit;
Thus the Clydesdale – see him go
To the field, the stud, the show!

Proper back, and ribs well-sprung,
Sound of limb and sound of lung;
Powerful loin and quarter wide,
Grace and majesty allied.

Basic power – living force –
Equine King – The Clydesdale Horse.

* * *

The dominant draught horse of English farms and farming was the Shire. Its ancestors carried knights into battle, and according to some historians it has its origins in the heavy horses introduced into Britain by the Normans after the Conquest. It was certainly descended from the English Great Horse of the Middle

Ages. After it was no longer required to carry knights in full armour into battle, its role changed to pulling coaches, carts and cannon across the English countryside. The roads in summer were little better than rough rutted tracks and in winter were deep in mud.

The Flanders horse, which was predominantly black in colour, was introduced into the Eastern Counties of England when Dutch contractors began to drain the Fens. When that work was finished the horses remained and were bred with the Great Horse, and the English draught horse came to be known as the English Black.

The modern Shire's foundation stallion is generally recognised to be Packington Blind Horse who stood at stud at Ashby de la Zouche between 1755 and 1770 and appears in the first Shire stud book. A large number of horses were claimed to be descended from him. The Cart Horse Society was formed in 1876 and the stud book opened two years later. The society was renamed the Shire Society in 1884.

The Shires of that time were much smaller than present-day animals being no more than 15 hands and resembling a heavy cob type of animal. The Shire horse of today is very different. It is the largest of the heavy horses. Stallions can stand up to 19 hands and mares up to 17 hands. It is a bulkier horse than the Clydesdale, with a dense round body with a broad back and strong loins, and will often weigh in excess of a ton. Seen in profile it has a Roman nose – unlike the Clydesdale. The neck although long for a draught horse is less long than the average Clydesdale neck. Black with white feathering is the most popular colour, but grey, bay and brown are also common.

Although some people think that the Shire and the

Clydesdale are two branches of the same breed, and there has been interbreeding over the years, it would be fair to say that the Shire is probably the heavier and more powerful and the Clydesdale has a better, more sure-footed action.

To give some idea of the power of the Shire horse, at the Wembley Exhibition Centre in 1924 a pair of Shires pulling against a machine for measuring mechanical power exceeded the maximum load on the machine and were estimated to be pulling a load of 50 tons. The same pair driven in tandem on slippery cobble stones moved over 18 tons.

The oldest of the heavy British horses is reputed to be the Suffolk Punch. Its origins are obscure. According to William Camden in his *Britannia* published in 1586, the Suffolk breed which he describes had existed for at least 80 years. What is not in doubt is that every Suffolk horse alive today can trace its descent in the direct male line to Thomas Crisp's Horse of Ufford which stood at stud in the Woodbridge area of Suffolk. The stallion was born around 1760. It was described as short legged (15.2 hands) with a large barrel-shaped body. It was chestnut in colour and all Suffolks are chestnut to this day. There are seven recognised shades: liver colour chestnut, dull dark chestnut, light mealy chestnut, red, golden, lemon and lastly bright chestnut. You have to have years of experience with Suffolk Punches to be able to distinguish the subtle differences in these colours.

The Suffolk Horse Society was formed in 1877. As a breed it belongs very firmly in the East Anglian countryside where it was always a favourite over the Shire and other heavy horses. This was due in part to the lack of feather on the legs which was a distinct advantage when ploughing on land with heavy clay soil.

The breed became famous for its docile nature and ability to work long hours on a ration that might have starved a Shire or Clydesdale. It matured early, which meant that many young Suffolks were put to light work at two, into full work at three and continued well into their mid-twenties.

The modern Suffolk stands at about 16 hands and often reaches 17 hands for a fully mature stallion. The hind legs are usually close together so that the horse can walk in a furrow, but unlike the Clydesdale, cow hocks are seldom seen. It has great width in front, which with its short legs gives it great direct pulling power. It was renowned for being capable of getting down on its knees to exert greater pressure on a dead weight. A mature horse is said to be capable of pulling two and a half times its own body weight. The great strength of the Suffolk Punch meant they were involved in pulling matches and competitions often held at agricultural shows. This match at Aldeham was typical:

This is to give notice that at the White Horse at Aldeham, on Friday the 18th of this instant June, will be given a silver cup of two guineas, to be drawn for by any team of horses, mares or geldings, and no less than two teams to draw for the said prize and they that make twenty of the best and fairest pulls and carry the weight over the block with the fewest tifters, according to the judgement of the proper persons, shall be instituted to the prize. Those that draw, to enter their names between the hours of ten and twelve on the day aforesaid, and the first team to be on the pin by three of the clock.

Pulling matches were very popular in East Anglia, and while they did not take the place of ploughing matches, they made for a bit of variety and the prize money was very welcome to an impoverished ploughman.

The Percheron heavy horse, which originated in the Perche region of Normandy, makes up the quartet of heavy horses which made such a large contribution to agriculture in the late 19th and early 20th centuries.

The original Percherons were the result of breeding between the native mares of the Perche region and Arab stallions. They were used as war horses, coach horses, and even as riding horses, as well as on the farm. They were a smaller and lighter version (15.2 hands) of the horse we know today. By the 17th century the horses of the Perche region were in great demand. By the 19th century the French Government had established a stud at Le Pin for the development of army remounts. In 1823, a stallion called Jean Le Blanc was foaled as a result of an outcross between a Percheron type mare and an Arab stallion named Gallipoly. All Percheron bloodlines trace directly back to this horse.

The modern Percheron is usually grey or black. Its gait is supple and active. The head is broad and square with a straight profile and a lively eye. The back is short and straight and very strong. The legs are short and clean and, like the Suffolk, without feathering which is why the breed found such favour in the Eastern Counties, working on heavy clay land. The average height today is about 16.2 hands, although the world's biggest horse was the United States Percheron, Dr Le Gear, who stood at 21 hands!

The Percheron became very popular in England after the

First World War as it was recognised for its adaptability to different climates and conditions. One of the men responsible for the animal being introduced into Cambridgeshire in the 1920s was HH Truman, a veterinary surgeon who was in practice in the town of March. He was awarded the Chevalier Du Merite Agricole by the French Government for services to the Percheron breed.

The Percheron would never have found much favour with a Scottish ploughman who could not see beyond the merits of the Clydesdale. However, they made a huge contribution to farming in East Anglia, and had they been introduced into Scotland at an earlier stage of their development, they would no doubt have become as revered and sung about as the Clydesdale.

Many horses which worked the land were undoubtedly cross bred as a lot of farmers could not afford to be fussy about the horses they bought so long as they could do the work. No doubt there were places in Scotland where the Highland Garron was used to pull the plough. And in England the Cleveland Bay found favour in some locations as it was smaller and more economical. But whatever the horsepower, the Horsemen cared for and worked their animals as if they were the best of the very best.

CHAPTER NINE

Harness and Implements

THE ADVANCE OF AGRICULTURE in Scotland and of the cause of the Secret Society of Horsemen were helped by three things: the improvement in the breeding of the heavy draught horse, the Napoleonic Wars which resulted in a huge demand and increase in agricultural output, and the invention of agricultural implements and improvement to equipment including horse harness.

It is natural when thinking of horse harness to suppose that it was made from leather and was similar to that which we recognise today. In poor country districts especially this was simply not the case, and in the 18th century equipment was made from very inferior material. A farming commentator of the time, George Culley, reported:

> I have in Scotland many times seen a horse and cart conveying peat's or turves, when the whole apparatus contained neither iron, leather nor hemp. The collar... was made of straw, the back band of plaited rushes, and the wheels of wood only, without bush of metal or binding of iron.

Henry Graham confirmed this state of affairs in *The Social Life of Scotland in the Eighteenth Century*:

The harness consisted of collars and saddles made of straw, and ropes made either from hair cut from horses' tails or rushes from which the pith has been stripped.

With equipment as poor as that, no matter the improvement in the breed of horse, little progress would have been made. In lowland or north-east Scotland, ploughs were drawn by oxen harnessed by a yoke system, or a mixture of oxen and horses, but rarely by horses alone. It was a horribly inefficient system in terms of both man and animal power and did a poor job of ploughing the land. The man at the stilts was solely concerned with steering the plough and holding it in the ground. Others were needed to lead the animals. Another man, the 'gadsman', drove the animals and urged them along with his pointed stick or 'gad'. The iron tip of an ox-gad dating from the 2nd century AD has been found in south-east Scotland. This was the type of equipment that was used by Robert Burns, with his brother Gilbert acting as gadsman.

Fortunately, by the beginning of the 19th century good harness made in leather started to become more commonly available. The main components of the equipment that harnessed a Clydesdale or Shire or Suffolk from the 1800s onwards, whether in Scotland or East Anglia, were the bridle, collar, saddle and breeching.

In an ideal world every horse had its own set of harness with a collar that fitted properly and harness that did not have to be adjusted from horse to horse according to what was needed. In the poorer ferm-touns this was inevitably often not the case as leather harness was expensive to buy. It was often second-hand, and much repaired.

The collar, which was put on the animal first before the bridle, was arguably the most important part of a working horse's harness as all the strength of the animal was transferred through the collar to the plough or whatever it was pulling. It was placed over the animal's head upside down or the wrong way up. This was necessary as all collars are wider at the throat than at the neck, and it has to be put on like that otherwise the animal would choke. Once over the head, the collar was rotated right way up and the mane smoothed down comfortably. Collars were heavy and got heavier the further north you travelled. They would weigh up to 14lbs in England and in Scotland were often double that. Many a young ploughman would struggle to lift a heavy collar over a Clydesdale's head, especially if the animal was lifting its head and being difficult.

The collar consisted of three parts stitched together. The body of the collar was densely padded with straw and covered by a thick woollen cloth usually with a check pattern and this lay against the horse's neck. The outside of this padding was covered in leather and was attached to the front of the collar or the roll which was a leather tube again packed with straw to make it rigid. The hames, which were made either from metal or wood, fitted into the groove between the roll and the body of the collar up each side of the horse's neck and formed a frame around the collar to which the ropes or chains from the implements were attached by means of hame hooks. Hames also had rings higher up the collar through which the reins were threaded on their way to the bridle and mouth bit. On some farms these hames were never removed from the collar, while on others they were removed every night, depending on the whim of the head Horseman.

The purpose of the bridle, of which there were many local patterns, was to keep the steel bit located in the correct position in the mouth. The bit was usually a straight metal bar with a ring on each side of the mouth; it was often hinged in the centre and called a snaffle bit. There were as many variations of bits as there were of bridles. It was vital that the bit fitted the mouth correctly – just in front of the molars and resting on the tongue. The control and guidance of the horse came through the reins in the ploughman's hands which were connected to the bit by means of the ring on either side of the mouth. Although many Horsemen with the Word prided themselves on controlling their pair without touching the reins, no-one would take an animal out to work without the bridle and bit in place. Horses could be unpredictable and even the quietest might bolt if confronted by something unknown. If a horse went out of control, the senior Horseman's advice would be to 'saw the heid', which meant to pull the reins hard, first one way then the other, as the best means of regaining control.

Many bridles, in addition to the usual brow-bands, nose-bands and throat lashes, had blinkers which allowed the horse forward vision only and stopped it being distracted by any peripheral activity which might cause it to bolt. These bridles in Scotland were called 'blin' bridles'.

If a horse was working with equipment with shafts, it had to wear a saddle which was held on by means of a girth strap and further anchored by the breeching straps ('britchin' in Scotland). These breeching straps, which ran over the backside and haunches of the horse, kept the saddle from slipping backwards or forwards when the load was going up or downhill or when the cart was being backed into the turnip shed. The saddle was made to take some weight from the cart through the shafts by means of a chain which ran over the saddle's central steel channel. This chain was connected to the top side of the cart shafts which had metal hoops for the purpose. Chains were also attached from the hame hooks on the collar to the same hoops on the shafts to provide forward propulsion for the implement. Because saddles had to take weight from the cart, they had to be well padded in a similar way to collars. The frame of the saddle, known as the tree, was usually made from beech or elm wood, and was attached to padding stuffed with straw and then covered by a leather housing. Across the tree at right angles to the horse's back ran the bridge or channel over which ran the back chain from one shaft to the other. It was essential for the welfare of the horse that the saddle fitted properly on its back and did not put pressure on the spine or withers which would result in sores and the horse not being able to be worked until they healed.

Each part of the horse harness depended on the other pieces in order to function properly and they were as interdependent as man was dependent on the horse. It was preferable for harness or tack to be kept in a separate tack room but on poorer farms this was not always possible. It was vital that such valuable equipment was kept in good repair, with the leather clean and supple. The men were expected to keep their horses' harness in good working order and many a keen young man would clean and polish his tack in his own time – late at night and by candle light. If the weather was very wet or the ground too hard with frost for ploughing, then the foreman would get the men to give all the harness a thorough clean. Each man would have his own tin of black polish and two brushes, one for applying the polish, the other for giving the leather a good shine, in much the same way that even today we look after good leather shoes.

Horsemen, of course, had special secret recipes for cleaning harness. One used in the north-east was typically complicated:

Ivory black, 1/2 lb
Bees wax, 1/4 lb
Indigo blue, 1oz
Turpentine, 1/2 pint
Heel ball, 1d
Spirit of Wine
Gum Arabic, 2 oz
Dissolve the wax in the Turpentine and the gum Arabic in the wine. Mix the blue and the black well together, simmer them all together in a few minutes and when used brush it on.

This type of recipe was common and worked well. I have been unable to discover what heel ball was but it was clearly important for the recipe.

For special occasions such as ploughing matches or horse shows, extra care and attention was lavished on harness. This special cleaning and burnishing of horse brasses would often start weeks before the event. A ploughman wanted his horses and harness to look the best not only for his own pride but because money and medals might be on offer for the best 'turn out'. Farmers were happy to foster this interest as harnesses that were well looked after would last longer and need to be repaired less often.

William Coutts of Tullienessle, Alford, was renowned for his presentation of show harness and had a long recipe list which included the following:

Paste for plated harness – 1lb precipitated chalk, 3 oz Spirit of turps, 1oz spirit of wine, 6 drm. Spirit of camphor, 3 drms. Liq. Ammonia.

Mix the fluids together, and then gradually stir in the chalk.

Horse brasses which were very important for special occasions received particular attention:

Paste for cleaning silver or brass – some well powdered bath brick, whiting, polishing paste for silver, candle grease, paraffin or turpentine. Heat slowly over a fire and keep stirring until all is into a paste. If too thick, just add a little more turpentine and paraffin until as thin as you wish it.

These cleaning recipes must have worked or they would not have been used.

Contemporary photographs show just how well horses were prepared for ploughing matches and how splendid they looked. They bear ample testimony to the men and the pride they took in their work and in their animals.

For centuries the old wooden plough – the twal-owsen – was the only plough in general use. It was a wooden mouldboard plough and was cumbersome and very heavy. The only metal pieces were the share, coulter, and cheek rack or bridle which were made of iron. Local ploughwrights built them, and although the design would have varied considerably from district to district, they all conformed to the same general pattern.

Teams of oxen or a mixed team of horses and oxen pulled the old ploughs. The more difficult the land the bigger the teams that were needed. In Berwickshire, for example, a common team would be four cattle and two horses. In Aberdeenshire up to twelve would be used, as the ground was that much harder to cultivate.

In about 1730 the Earl of Stair introduced to Scotland a Dutch plough for which a patent was secured, and at the same time a similar plough called the Rotherham was introduced in England. However, neither of these really took on in Scotland.

The first plough that could be pulled successfully using only two horses was invented by James Small who was born in Berwickshire in 1741. It was called the Small's Chain or Swing plough and the design rapidly gained favour. James Small was apprenticed as a ploughwright and blacksmith at Hutton in Berwickshire where he used his skills to the limit. He was not only very good at his craft, he also had an enquiring and observant mind. He went to England for a time to work at his trade and became aware of the Rotherham and the Dutch plough designs. When he returned to Scotland he settled at Blackadder Mount and began experimenting with his own designs. His plough would have a feathered share and a curved, instead of a straight, mouldboard. Iron was to displace wood in the vital parts – the mouldboard, the sheath and the head – giving the plough more strength but less bulk and weight. He did repeated trials to get the shape of the mouldboard and share just right to cut the furrow and turn the sod over. He went about it from the outset in a very scientific way by using spring balances to measure the draught and soft wooden mouldboards to show how friction could be evened out and reduced. Having worked out the shape he wanted, he took his design to the Carron Iron Works at Falkirk where the working parts were cast in iron. The result was the curved mouldboard which is to be seen on ploughs to this day.

Small stated that his plough was made according to basic mechanical principles, and he analysed these in his book, *A Treatise on Ploughs* (1784). The advantage of Small's plough was immediate, with only two horses being required to pull it. Not everyone could work the plough initially and Small had to train both men and horses.

At a competition at Dalkeith, spectators were amazed to see one man and two horses do a much better job than was possible with the old plough with its team of four men and eight to twelve oxen. News of his invention quickly spread and even reached the King, and Small was called south to demonstrate the virtues of the new machine.

Small realised just how much his plough was of benefit to farms and farming, but being an altruist he would not take out any patents to protect his design. The result was that blacksmiths everywhere copied his plough, assisted by his first book and then by his second, *Ploughs and Wheeled Carriages*. Small may have died a poor man in 1793 at the age of 53 but he was aware of the huge contribution he had made to agriculture. By 1794 in Alloa all the ploughs at a ploughing match were Small's design.

Constant improvements and adaptations were made to the original design. For instance, Wilkie added a furrow wheel which helped steady it. An important development was the use of replaceable parts. Moveable point shares and detachable feathers and tailpieces were made, and boards tended to become shorter. The skim was substituted for the knife coulter which allowed dung to be effectively turned in. Eventually, plough making became the work of specialist factories.

The new plough caused a complete revolution in farming. Land which could not easily be ploughed by the old teams was drained, cleared and ploughed. Cultivation was possible over a much larger area and could be done with less man-power. One man and his pair of horses could plough up to 50 acres of average arable land. Before the Small plough, anyone and everyone would give a hand with the ploughing. Now a skilled man was required, both with machinery and in the way of horses. He was called the Horseman and it was Horsemen who formed the Secret Society of Horsemen.

The first job in the morning on a ferm-toun was grain threshing which was also done whenever the weather caused the cessation of ploughing. The old time-honoured way, which was very slow and labour intensive, was to use a flail to batter the corn sheaves to separate the grain and chaff from the stalks. This was then winnowed – the grain and chaff were tossed in the air, either outside where there was a good wind or between opposite open barn doors with a good through draft. The wind blew away the chaff leaving the heavier grain behind.

The first winnowing machine in Scotland was built by James Meikle who had been sent to Holland to study Dutch farming methods by his employer, Andrew Fletcher of Saltoun. The winnowing machine worked well but was condemned out of hand by the Calvinist Church authorities of the time as it was thought to be the work of the Devil and to interfere with the laws of God to produce what was called the 'Devil's wind'.

Andrew, the son of James Meikle, made the first efficient threshing machine. His first effort fell to bits, but in 1786 he built another and it worked. The sheaf of corn was fed through fluted rollers to a revolving drum which was equipped with beaters to knock out the grain. At first there was no arrangement to separate the straw from the chaff and grain. Meikle may have made a revolving rake to draw away the straw, but others claimed to have invented this device. Meikle, like Small, did not take out a patent on his machine and profited very little by his invention, and it is recorded that a public subscription was raised to provide some money for his old age.

Most threshing mills in Scotland were initially powered by water; in England threshing machines were almost all portable, owned by contractors and powered by steam engines.

The last great invention which made life so much more productive for the farmer and eased the burden on the farm-worker was the reaper. This in turn led to the binder and eventually in our time to the combined threshing machine and reaper – the combine harvester.

The man who invented a reaper on the principles that are still used today was called Patrick Bell. He was a divinity student and a farmer's son. One day in 1826 he saw a pair of shears sticking out of a hedge and had a flash of inspiration. He built his machine in secret and tried it out in a barn away from prying eyes in case it didn't work. But it did! He tried it once more, outside and at dusk, again for reasons of secrecy. This time it failed because he had forgotten an essential feature, but as soon as he realised his mistake and rectified it, the machine worked well.

A public trial of the reaper was held and the *Quarterly*

Journal of Agriculture gave a favourable report. The Highland Society awarded Bell £50 which only just covered his expenses. Bell, like the others before him, did not take out a patent and it was left to country blacksmiths to make the machine, but they were not very successful. Some machines were sent abroad and detailed descriptions were published in various magazines, and the result was that three years later McCormick in the USA produced a reaper incorporating some of the Bell principles.

The American reaper, instead of using the principle of scissors to cut the grain, had a saw-toothed straight blade, supported by fingers working backwards and forwards. It was soon being produced in factories and the Bell machine was neglected. However, when the McCormick machine was exhibited at Crystal Palace, someone remembered Bell's reaper which was still in use on his brother's farm. A contest was staged and the Bell machine won! However, new and improved reapers soon beat the somewhat cumbersome Bell.

As for Bell himself, he completed his studies to be a minister and took a parish at Carmyle in Angus. He was totally indifferent to fame and fortune, and public recognition came late. In 1868, forty years after his first invention, the Highland and Agricultural Society presented him with a plate and £1,000.

In the meantime, the best features of the rival machines were combined. Instead of the grain being delivered, devices were adopted where two men on the machine could lay the grain ready for the sheaves to be hand bound. This was soon changed to a self-delivery type and the binder (as we who are old enough to remember it) was born. It was a heavy machine which got bogged down very readily in a wet field and always needed three good horses to pull it, but it made an enormous contribution towards helping to meet the hugely increased demand for grain to feed the ever growing population.

The revolution in agriculture and agricultural machinery eventually led to the production of efficient tractors which by the early 1950s were taking the place of the working pair of horse. The arrival of the tractor coincided with the winding up of most of the Secret Societies. Horsemen were converted into tractor drivers, and while many were sad to see the end of the horse era, many were not. I remember being quite exultant at home on our farm when the last horse – a chestnut Clydesdale gelding called Sam – left and was replaced by the little grey Ferguson tractor. Our ploughman Jake welcomed these changes just as much as I did. Although he never said so, I'm sure his opinion coincided with that of the farm worker who was asked whether he liked his new tractor:

'Oh it's great!'

'Don't you miss the horses?'

'Na na, I walked a'hint a pair of fartin' horses far oo'er long!'

CHAPTER TEN

Physical Restraint of Horses

FROM THE TIME HORSES were first domesticated they were restrained by means of ropes made from all manner of natural materials – horsehair and leather were most common, but other materials such as plant fibres from broom or heather may have been used. Horses were caught and retained by a simple loop around the neck, which, if the animal was being difficult and fighting the tether, had the potential to cause it to choke, sometimes with fatal consequences.

The halter, which fits around the head of the animal, gets round the problem of choking. It is the most basic requirement for tying up the animal and leading it out in hand. Halters were invariably made from hemp rope, usually adjustable so that one halter could quickly be adapted to fit horses with different head sizes. Most heavy horses were tied up in a stable stall with a halter, with the shank of the rope fed through a ring attached to the edge of the manger and then tied to a block of wood about four inches in diameter. The end of the halter was knotted underneath the block, or sinker, as it was called in some parts of the country. This arrangement allowed the animal some movement backwards and forwards in its stall. It also meant that in an emergency such as a fire, the animal could be quickly released by cutting the rope. If chains were used for tying up, as they are in cow byres, there was not the same possibility of quick release.

Young horses on a halter could be prone to rearing in the

stable but were cured of this vice fairly readily. The following 'cure' came from the Buchan area:

> Take a rope 15 feet long, throw it over his back, reach under his body, take hold of the end of the rope and tie an ordinary slip knot. Have this knot exactly below the horse's belly. Advance this rope through his forelegs then through the halter and hitch to the ring in the manger, do not hitch the halter rope.

This is a simple, clever, straight-forward solution to a tricky problem. The young horse will be unable to rear due to the restraint of the rope around its girth which is attached to the manger. To a non-Horseman, the obvious remedy for stopping an animal rearing in the stable would be to tie it up very short by the halter to the manger, but this might well worsen the problem by making the animal head shy.

The bridle, the primary means of physical restraint in the horse, contains the bit which is directly linked to the man behind by the reins. By pulling on the reins, the ploughman will tell the horse to go left or right, stop or go forward.

Before the bit was invented the ancient horsemen used damaging nose rings and lip rings to guide and restrain. Bits varied in severity over the centuries with the Romans in particular using severe pieces of metal in the mouth to control war-horses in battle. This trend continued in medieval times, but heavy horses pulling a plough or a cart normally only required a simple straight metal bar as a bit, or at most a snaffle bit hinged in the middle.

The halter and the bridle were, and still are, the physical methods of restraint and control, but there were circumstances where normal methods were not sufficient to subdue an unruly animal. Although Horsemen of the Secret Society had many secret methods of subjugating and controlling horses, principally by using the horse's sense of smell, this is not the whole story. Many Horsemen faced with difficult and potentially violent animals would resort to physical methods of restraint.

Horsemen used the fact that the horse has a very sensitive muzzle as a means to control a difficult or nervous animal. An instrument called a twitch was a short piece of wood such as a pick-axe handle with a cord loop at one end. Modern equivalents made of metal are still used. When the loop was placed around the horse's nose and twisted tight, in most cases the animal would go into what appeared to be a trance-like state and allow procedures to be carried out that it would not allow if the twitch had not been applied.

A twitch was especially useful for controlling nervous young horses having their feet trimmed or shod for the first time. The procedure generally worked well, but just occasionally a horse would go crazy when a twitch was applied tightly, and the whole procedure would have to be abandoned as the situation could become very dangerous for the Horseman holding the instrument.

It used to be thought the twitch worked by distracting the animal from whatever was being done to it by applying a different type of pain. However, recent studies have shown that the nose is an acupuncture point and the root of many nerve endings. Applying a twitch has been shown to cause the release of endorphins. These are natural morphine-like substances which are pain relieving as well as calming chemicals. The Horsemen didn't know how or why the twitch worked, but that didn't matter – it worked, and it was one of their techniques. It wasn't a secret and is still used today.

A twitch was sometimes applied to the ear of the horse, as the ear is another very sensitive part of the horse's anatomy. Other strange implements have been applied to the ear of a difficult horse. Charles Gardiner from Diss in Norfolk has described how his father around the time of the First World War used a metal ring and wax thread with a bead on the end to quieten recalcitrant horses. The metal ring was placed over the horse's ear and the waxed thread with a bead on one end dangled inside the ear. This was removed and re-placed over a period of several hours and was said to calm the wildest of animals. He didn't say was how he got the ring and bead in place to begin with! Other people have used the horse's ear much like an acupuncture point. It has been said that sticking a hat-pin through the tip of one ear will calm an unsettled horse and help it work well all day – so long as the pin is in place!

An old trick known to the Greeks and the Romans was the use of a blindfold to calm a horse, and its use and usefulness was passed down through the ages. In medieval times a piece of equipment known as a closed bridle or a blind headstall was common. A piece of canvas was placed between the cheek pieces, nose-band and brow-band which effectively blocked the animal's vision, and it became totally reliant on its handler. This device was used in medieval riding schools. Very vicious horses, usually stallions, were sometimes intentionally blinded in order to protect the grooms who were handling them. This was a barbaric practice, but in medieval England, where everyday violence was a fact of life, it was hardly worth comment. Fortunately for horses this type of practice was a thing of the past by the time the Secret Society of Horsemen was being formed.

Horsemen knew how effective a blindfold could be. One source from the north-east of Scotland states:

If they are dangerous and not fit for handling, take a cover in your arms, when he makes a race at you, throw this cover over his head then you can venture up beside him, you must give him a lot of handling, then you require to rary [control] him.

Another Horseman wrote in much the same way:

When he makes a race at you, throw a cover over his head and go up to him. You must give him a good deal of work then.

It sounds simple and effective common sense, but for all that it would take a brave man and one very sure of himself to stand his ground and get his aim right with the blindfold when confronted by a horse that intended to inflict damage either with its teeth or feet. Fortunately for Horsemen, most draught horses unless provoked or frightened were quiet phlegmatic beasts.

Much more common was the horse that was prone to kicking

– usually with the back feet. They were often nervous beasts or ones had been badly handled in their formative years. They were tolerated by farmer owners – who, after all, were less likely to be damaged by flying hooves than ploughmen – as many highly strung horses were often good willing workers once they were safely yoked to a plough or cart.

A Horseman could do a lot to reduce the risk of being kicked and to cure an animal of kicking. His methods were usually called recipes (or archaically 'receipts') in much the same way that medical treatments were called recipes and many are recorded in old notebooks. Some sound hard and cruel:

> The art of breaking a horse from kicking: take a cord and tie it round his body, rack it tight and lead your cord to his jaw bone and tail or you may tie them round the bullocks [buttocks] or fitlocks [fetlocks] and nose, you may use wire or cord. The vice of a horse lies in its head, the last thing you can try if cord won't do is the ear or nose put two drops of the oil of Ambegerus [ambergris?] on two knots and put (or pat) it into his ear, then put a little oil or originam [origanum?] in his nostrils or oil of fennel and oil of Arron, 1/4 of digitalis or black drops from 25 to 40.

It is difficult to imagine a more severe method to stop kicking and I can hardly think the chemical method would ever be required or that it would be effective.

Other recipes that don't seem so severe include:

For kicking in the stable: you require four shackle belts
with the D in the centre of each. Put one on each leg of
the horse then take short lines in a crossed form and
fixed to the D's on your belts. Then make the horse kick
until he realises resistance is non effective.

This sounds very effective and much more humane. A kicking
horse will rapidly tire of attempting to lash out when it is
restrained in this manner.

Many horses which are otherwise well mannered in the stable
will sometimes play up when being groomed. In two different
notebooks the recipes for coping with this problem were almost
identical and again very severe:

You require to strap up the foreleg then take a line and
fix it to his lower jaw. Advance this line back to the post
of his traves [travise or trevis] then pull it up tight, then
you can walk around him in safety.

The traves is the division between the stalls in the stable and it
is not difficult to see that even the most recalcitrant of horses would
have a problem in attacking a groom when tied up in this way.

Getting up alongside a horse in a stall when it was liable to
kick was not an easy matter for an inexperienced man.
Horsemen had the answer:

Take a handkerchief and put some smelling stuff on it
and throw it up beside the horse, but only half way up,
so he will have to come to the end of his rope to smell

it, go up beside him then and have some of the same smelling stuff on your hand and rub his nose with it, you will easily get up beside him again.

A horse that kicked in the stable was a nuisance, one that kicked while ploughing or when harnessed to a cart was an economic liability as it might damage equipment, and was liable to be treated quite harshly. It was also more public, and a Horseman would not like to be embarrassed by a horse of which he was clearly not in control:

Receipt [recipe] for kicking in the cart.
Take two plough lines, fix to the lower jaw on each side of the mouth, then bring them back to the D's in your britchen [breeching harness over the hindquarters] and fix them down one on each shaft, this will cause him to punish himself when he resists.

Kicking in the plough was regarded more seriously than kicking in the cart and a variety of physical methods were used to stop this:

The Art of breaking a horse kicking in the plough.
Buck the tail in the third link, or put a rope round its waist then tie another to its hind legs, then bring it forward through the rope around its waist, then through its forelegs then tie it down with a missie [rope] in its mouth or rack its waist with a rope.

Another way to stop them kicking in the plough, get a good stick and whenever they start to kick, strike them on the sennon [tendon] in the hind legs above the knee, on the outside, watch the one that goes furthest out, and keep going hardest at it till it stops.

The above recipes came from the same Horseman. Another Horseman had different recipes to counter the same problem:

Receipt for kicking in the plough.

Take two plough lines; fix one to the lower jaw and above the nostrils. Before doing so, you need two men to manage this, one to each line, you must fight him till he is panting for breath, if he still resists you must repeat the dose until he is thoroughly subdued. Another receipt for the same you require two shackle belts on his hind legs then put a line around his middle, then take another line and pass it through the rings on your bridle, then advance it through the horse's forelegs, then to the middle, then fix one to each belt, you can easily work them in this fashion.

Yet another man had a very different solution:

To break a horse kicking in the theats [plough traces].

Get a key and rack one of its lugs. Put it beneath the head stool of the bridle so as no one will see it, or tie a strong rope to both the hind legs, then bring it forward under the belly band of your theats, then tie it to both the forelegs at the paster [pastern] joints. Tie it in the same place behind, give them room to travel no more, with this on. Or get a silk pock [pouch?] put a lead ball in it and tie the mouth of it with a silk thread. Tie it to the mane, then put it into its lug [ear]. This should stop them.

This should stop it kicking all right just so long as it didn't send it into a frenzy!

These recipes all come from notebooks written by Scottish ploughmen. Their equivalents can easily be found south of the Border. The following is from a Suffolk Horseman's notebook as described by George Ewart Evans:

To Still the horse from Kicking by Druging him.

Drop 4 or 5 drops of ... into his ear, or make a nott of tow and drop a few drops of the essence of ... on it; and put it in his ear. And oil of rhodium up his nostrils and the oil of asp.

Or put 5 drops of ... in each ear. Will make him work kindly.

Another method described is very similar to the key method but instead uses a gagging iron. This was a small oval metal device usually made by the local blacksmith. A kicking horse would have a thin strong cord passed through its mouth and up the side of his head. There it was attached to the gagging iron which was concealed under the bridle. By pulling on the cord it was possible to exert considerable pressure on the animal by way of the gag to stop any misbehaviour.

Some horses either through laziness or just to be difficult would not pull properly through the collar. The remedies for this type of bad behaviour varied, depending on whether the horse was working on its own or as one of a pair:

Recipe for taking the collar.

If your horse won't push to the collar, fix a line to his lower jaw, then take a wisp of straw and fix the line to it, then advance it through your collar, you require then to take the collar in your arms, and stand above the straw, this will prevent your horse from throwing you.

This doesn't quite make sense, although the essence of what the man was saying just about comes through. He may have meant that the horse would not allow the collar to be placed over its head which may have been due to it being smeared with pig or toad blood by a rival in which case the remedy was to rub the collar all over with horse dung. You might even have retaliated by stopping the rival's horse from leaving the stable by blowing pig's blood up its nose whereupon it would not go out. The remedy to reverse the effect of the blood was to blow pepper or snuff up the nose, and the horse will then sneeze and be prepared to move again.

A more obvious and barbaric treatment for making an animal work was the following:

Receipt for horse in front cart.

Take a small stop or brog [tack] not exceeding one fourth of an inch, take it in your hand, stob behind the foreleg where you will find a large vein. Few horse will resist this mode of treatment – if the above receipt fails you can make a scratch in the breast of your horse which will cause the blood to flow, then put 5 drops of turpentine into the wound, immediately afterwards use whip and make it slightly strike the wound.

Such treatment would make any horse move just to get away from the smarting pain.

When a horse would not pull and relied on the other horse to do all the work, the following was recommended:

Receipt for a bad worker.

If your horse refuses to draw in cart, take a plough line and tie it to his lower jaw, then advance to the draught of your first (willing) horse and keep hold of your line in your hand, and then start the horse in front, this will cause him to get a severe check.

A recipe for a bad worker which did not have another horse harnessed in trace, i.e. in front of the reluctant worker, is the following:

Take a short line and place a loop on the end of it – then pass it over the nostrils, then draw it tight, which will enclose its breath, when the horse advances slip the line.

As a device it was cunningly clever and bound to work on most horses. Whether it was welfare friendly was another matter.

These devices or recipes were hard enough but not as bad as the following:

If you have a horse that will not work in the cart, take a piece of small stick and put it in his ear then take a heavier stick and give the small one a stroke and I think your horse will move; if that does not lift him try a fussie [phosphorus] match in ear or in his flank but watch yourself.

Hopefully the above recipe, although it came from a Society member's notebook, was not one used by a whisperer. If it was, and the rest of his group knew about the practice, I hope they showed him the error of his ways.

Some remedies were much less severe. James Nimmo had two cures which would seem to work well:

One of the best cures for a setter [reluctant worker] is to strap up one of his forelegs, when after standing for a while on three legs, the animal is generally as willing to start as the person who has him in charge. Another cure for setting is to fasten a ring on top of the britchin, get a piece of new, hard, plough rein, pass it through the ring and in below the horse's tail, bring it back again through the ring, then take an end of the rein in each hand and pull first with one hand and then with the other. Thus a sawing sort of motion is created, which the horse finds so disagreeable that he starts off at a trot or gallop to leave his tormentor behind.

Not all horses that were considered difficult were reluctant to pull. Some – especially youngsters – were too enthusiastic and pulled too hard. This could be dangerous and had to be curbed:

Receipt for fast going horse.

Take hold of the reins of your bridle and place your finger betwixt his jaws by doing so he becomes obedient to your will.

Receipt for fast going horse in the plough:

You require a rod not exceeding 6 inches in length with cross bar in the centre – with a ring in each end of it, ring at neither cross bar. You take this rod and fix it to the rings of your bridle. This bar betwixt his jaws then you require a line fixed to the lower ring of your rod, by this agreement you can steady him if he becomes restive.

The quote is taken verbatim from the Horseman's notebook, and although it is not too clear exactly what he means, clearly he is advocating a more severe type of bit which will give more control. While a severe bit may well be effective, many old Horsemen said the best cure for a young keen horse was another in harness with it. An older, quieter animal would let the young one do all the hard pulling work to begin with. This soon tired it out and it learned its lesson very quickly.

Most of the training of a young horse, after the initial hurdle of getting it used to harness, was done in a pair with an older, wiser horse – often its mother if she was available. Training and breaking young horses to harness was a job for the most experienced of Horsemen. It could be dangerous, and unless done properly could result in permanent damage to the animal – if not the handler. Robert Dempster of Alyth had some good advice on the subject:

When breaking the colts always secure the services of a good man. At present any goslin [youngster] gets this to do, and they are generally a torture to themselves and whoever has to do with them afterwards. Get the colt into a shed or loose-box, halter them with a halter that won't run tight on the jaws. If you have one of the buckling brechams it will be handy but always slip it over the head, making it tighter as the colt learns to push. When you put on the bridle open the jaws with the thumb into the wick of the mouth, do the same taking it out – be very cautious for a long time when putting on the harness. Give them a lunge with a long rein first to the right and then to the left, which lets you know what strength they have in the head. Give them a slip or stick [a sleeper or heavy log] to draw to begin with. A good man can make the best job if he has a double sledge for them, and when they are cousened. Having a plough brought, just bring the swingletrees [the cross piece in front of the plough to which the plough traces are harnessed] to it, give then a number of rounds, not too deep to begin with; give good round turns till they are aquaint with the swingletrees and chains at their heels. It is best not to have the tie hooks attached to the bits for some time but to have a halter below the bridle to begin with.

At this point in the training young horses would learn the words of command which varied from district to district and between countries. Common words were 'back', 'stand', 'go on' and 'go steady' in England, and 'hi', 'whissh' and 'whoa' or, even more urgent, 'hup', 'haud' and 'back back' in Scotland.

The basics of walking, trotting and standing had to be taught and the following recipe shows just how it could be done:

> First you require the waist belt with three Ds on each side, then you take two plough lines, fix one on either side of his lower jaw, then advance them through the Ds of your waist belt. Then go behind your horse with the lines in your hand, carrying your whip in your other hand, the lines are your regulators, you can tell them to walk, trot or stand if he refuses you must whip him until he obeys. You can also learn your horse a sort of language that you wish by going behind your horse with a line in each hand by pulling it to any point by using a fixed term or expression and you horse will soon learn to obey you.

A young and spirited animal would sometimes disobey by rearing. This was often seen as the worst type of dangerous bad behaviour. As you would expect, there was a recipe for curing it:

> To Cure a Horse from Rearing.
>
> Get a pretty strong strap of leather with a buckle attached on one end, fasten on two bits of wood, each about three quarters of an inch thick, the distance between the two pieces of wood to be the exact breadth

of the bridge of a horse's nose. Then take a piece of cord and fasten it to the strap so as to make a halter, tighten the strap by means of a buckle and each piece of wood will press slightly above the horse's nostril; you have now only to fasten a piece of rope to the strap, and tie the other end to the girth or circingle. With this contrivance a horse will never succeed in rearing.

Part of the training for a young Suffolk Punch was to teach it to go down on its knees in order to exert its full strength in a dead pull. The following comes from the diary of a Suffolk Horseman:

To Learn a Young Horses Game of Drawing.

First learn him to go down on his knees. Then put him in a long pair of traice. Chain him to a tree. Take the traice off the shoulder hook. Tie a piece of cord on each side of the bit and tie it to the traice. Touch his flank and his knees till he go down. Then whip him over the wallows till he draw kindly. Give him comfort and coax him on the neck with the whip. And give him a little corn and leave him with a feed of corn.

Horsemen were very jealous of their reputation and would not knowingly be seen inflicting any kind of harm or physical restraint on a horse, even on the most difficult and vicious. We know now that physical methods were used, mostly unwillingly. The ultimate sanction to be used on a very dangerous animal was to cast it. This was to make it lie down against its will, which had the effect normally of making it subservient to the Horseman's will. As a technique it would be repeated if required and was usually done in great secrecy by a group of Horsemen who would travel to a farm at the request of a brother Horseman. The following method of casting a horse comes from the north-east:

> Take your horse when the ground is soft, if they are youngsters, you require knee-caps, one shackle belt for the aft foreleg with a D in the centre (aft fore-leg is the one on the opposite side of the horse from your self). Second you require another belt – this to strap up a near fore-leg. Third you require a girth belt with three Ds, one on each side and another beneath the belly, the side Ds stand for other purposes. Fourth then take a line and pass it through the belly, then advance to the aft fore leg and fix it to the D in your belt.
>
> Fifth strap up your near fore-leg, then take hold of your line in your hand, then you require another man with a deaf whip to whip him up. When he springs keep the line quite tight, that will cause him to come to his knees, but you must whip him up until he lies down on his own accord, then clap him and coax him. You require to have your hand scented with the oil of aniseeds, then use your whip and stand behind his shoulder and crack your whip above his ears until he will lie down without any motion if he offers to resist you must let him up and repeat the dose.

As a technique it looked fairly foolproof, but it required a fair amount of equipment and several sturdy helpers.

Another method was much more straightforward and only

required a good, long, thick rope. This was divided into two equal parts and a loop made at one end. The loop was passed over the animal's head and the two strands were then taken back under the chest and abdomen to the hind legs where each length was passed around each pastern, crossed over on itself so that each formed a loop around the pasterns. Both ends were then taken back through the looped end, which was round the neck. A man on each end of the rope would pull backwards while a man at the front controlled the head with a halter. When the horse started to go down the man at the head would force it to the ground and sit on it. With the head on the ground the horse could not rise and the men with the ropes would tie the legs to put a stop to further kicking. It was a simple technique requiring only three men but was not without risk. I have seen it working albeit on a horse that was already sedated.

Having read the many variations of the Horseman's Oath which all state in one way or another that you must never 'bad use a horse or see them bad used', it is difficult to see how someone who has taken such an oath could in all conscience condone some of the physical methods that were used on horses. However, this must be viewed in the context of the times. What might be seen as a welfare issue in the 21st century would not be considered in any way cruel in the 18th and 19th centuries. Some of the restraints seem to modern eyes severe and hard, but to men of those times would not be so regarded. If the Horsemen were secretive about their methods, it was more to promote the myth that whispering and the Word were the means by which they managed and controlled their horses, rather than to conceal methods that might be thought cruel.

CHAPTER ELEVEN

The Toasts They Made and The Songs They Sang

UNTIL THE LATE 1930S many thousands of single men worked on Scottish and English farms. In Scotland most were housed in primitive communal bothies or chaumers on the farm. Their work was hard and the weather conditions could often be severe, but strong bonds were formed between Horsemen and the animals which shared their work and living conditions. There was, after all, often only a thin partition between the men and their horses.

Unlike their contemporaries in England who mostly lived in villages, it was difficult for Scottish ploughmen to have much of a social life. Their living conditions probably accounted for the firm hold the Secret Society of Horsemen had over most farms. Members of the Society formed a brotherhood to protect one other against the worst conditions. Of course, it wasn't all misery, and the men in the bothies made their own entertainment. Secret meetings of Society members were often an excuse for drinking sessions which were punctuated by toasts and bothy ballads.

Most of the toasts have gone unrecorded until now, but I have been given access to many which were written down in notebooks. The following come from a notebook from Angus and were no doubt common throughout the district. The spellings are original:

1. There's to them that brought me here. There's to them that brought me thighter. There's to them that brought me here and changed my name from friend to brother and for their sake I will drink this glass and for the companies sake I will drink another.

2. There's to the horse with the three white feet the chestnut tail mane [chestnut tail and mane] there's to the man that caught the first horse his name was Cuble Cain.

3. There's to the horse that I do drive oft times against me they do strive but if they do they are sure to rue little do they know what a man can do.

4. There's to the horse that I knocked down with one effectual blow he rises up and smiles at me and asks me where to go.

5. There's to the lips that can keep a secret.

6. There's to the 3 Cs Corn Clean Clap.

7. There's to the oak the best of wood. The wildest horse that ever stood the wildest mare that ever ran was managed both by men or man.

8. There's to the horse that goes in the theats and never lets them slack consider well before you strike for fear he that he strikes back.

9. There's to the 3 Ps Practice Patience and Perseverance.

10. There's to the 3 Hs Horse, Hemp & Harness.

11. There's to the whip, the plough, there's to the cart the saddle, theres to the bonnie lad that carrys the key to the stable.

12. There's to yon high mountain, there's to yon low lying glen where they train young horses and teach young men.

13. There's to the horse with the three white feet that stands well up in his manger he knows the crack of his masters whip and cares not for the voice of a stranger.

14. There's to the horse that I love best, there's to the cord that bound him there's to the brother that can meet one another from top to bottom sound him.

15. There's to you for as good as you are. There's to me for as bad as I am for as good as you are for as bad as I am.

16. There's to the two beautiful animals that goes before man teach them and train them till they both go as one. [reference to the Word.]

17. There's to the four on the land six in the dum in the middle and all goes as one [reference to the Word].

18. There's to the bonnie blues that goes before man take them and try them and make them go as one [reference to the Word].

Most of the toasts were written in the form of a rhyme. Here are more, some set as riddles, all of which originated in the north-east. To the best of my knowledge, they have never been published before:

There's to the BH, the BC and N
that was first brought here by a show,
Now if you'll tell me the meaning of the BH, the BC and N.
I'll trust you with all I know.

(BH, BC and N = Brown Horse, Bob Cowans and Nicholsons.)

There's to the man that can conceal,
And keep a thing well hidden
Bring both to his horse to the crack of the whip
And stand like a stone when bidden.

There were many variations to this toast:

There's to the yoke that our forefathers broke and there's to
The horse that was kitten,
There's to The horse that yielded to the stroke
And stands like a stone when bidden.

There's to the man, and none but he,
Can work his horse by the rule of three;
By the crack of his whip or the wave of his hand
He can make them either go or stand.

There's to the horse with the three white feet
And there's to the cord that bound him,
When as brothers they meet one another
From top to bottom they sound him.

The following seems to be a common riddle:

As I came out this moonlight night
To view your meetings earlie

I came to try and to be tried
And hope you'll try me fairly.
(Answer)
Young man no doubt you're a stranger here,
Your name I'll no deny,
But ere we part this moonlight night,
Your courage I will try.

There's to the horsemen, the horsemen of night,
Who trains his horse at dead of night;
He learns them to walk, he learns them to stand,
He learns them to obey the word of command.

There's to the yoke our forefathers broke,
And there's to the plough that was hidden,
There's to the horse that can pull
And stand like a stone when bidden.

There's to yon twa lovely animals
That go before man;
I'll take them and try them
And make them go as one. [A reference to The Word.]

There's to the horseman, who he be,
He works his horse by rule of three,
He makes them go or makes them stand
By the crack of his whip or the wave of his hand.

There's to the BH that was brought here for show,
There's to the BH the HM and J
If you tell me the meaning of that,
I'll trust you with all I know.

There's to them that can work horses,
Bad luck to them that's cruel,
Let perseverance be their guide
And nature be their rule.

There's to the horse with three W feet,
The chestnut main and tail
There's to the man that broke him in,
His name was Juble Cain.

'There's to the bee theat makes the honey, the poor man
works the work and the Masters pocket the money.'

Question: In which or where, a horse or mare, does your
secret letters lie?

Answer: A mare in foal.

When the sun does set into the west
And our horse begins to slumber
Since we are here together met
Who can tell our number?
(ENO)
ENO is ONE backwards, which is of course the Horseman's
Word!

There's to the horse that draws in the theats
And never draws a slack
Speak twice to him before you strike
In case he strikes you back.

There's to the horse, the braw black horse,
And there's to the cords that bind him
And there's to the brother that meets a brother
And conquers and combines him.

There's to the horse with the star on his brow,
There's to the mare with the bell on her breast
They're easy to harness and canny to yoke,
They're a braw gain pair that keeps time on the clock.

I can toss an orange of an apple
And through the form of friendship
I'll drink of this and if you are a man
I took you to be, for this glass and thank me
I can toss an apple of an orange
And through the form of friendship
I'll drink of thee and if I am a man
You took me to be, for this glass I'll thank thee
(If he cannot answer you)
You fool, you fool, you silly fool,
I thought you were a man
But since you cannot answer me
Give it to one who can.

There's to all the Horseman lads
That's bound by Horsemen ties
Never abuse nor yet bad – use
The horses that you drive
There's to yon high mountains
And yon dreary plains
Where we train our horses
And teach young men.

Some toasts are written from the horse's point of view, indicating the closeness between man and horse.

A Horse's Petition to His Master or *A Horse's Prayer*

Going up the hill, whip me not
Down the hill hurry me not,
On the level, spare me not
Nor in the stable forget me not.
Of clean water, stower me not
With sponge or brush, neglect me not.
Tired or hot, chill me not,
With bit or rein, jerk me not
And when you're angry, strike me not.

The following verse is rather maudlin:

Weep not for me ye horsemen lads,
Though low you see me lie,
There's many a brawer horse than me

Been brought out here to die.
You've fed me well, you've clad me well,
It's you I do adore,
So fare ye well ye horseman lads,
I'll never see you more.

The vast majority of the toasts and verses composed and recited by the ploughmen reflected their interest in their horses, drinking and women:

Through mire and clay I've trod all day
Behind they twa auld bees,
Now night is night and I am dry
I think I'll drink of this.

Now I have drunk to no extent,
Nor have I drunk in vain,
For fear I don't get anymore
I think I'll taste again.

For liquor is a flowing cup,
Its like a floating ball:
For fear I don't get any more
I think I'll drink it all.

Now I have drunk to no extent,
Nor have I drunk in vain
But if you want another toast
Just fill it up again.

And of course women were never very far away from a young man's mind:

There's the to the rings, the bonnie bridle rings,
The rings that should ne'er be forgot
There's to the man, the well-tempered man
That can tie the Horseman's knot.
There's to the Horsemen and the Horseman's bairns,
There's no [not] a maid with her lovely charms,
But what likes to lie in her Horseman's arms.

There's to the jolly ploughman lad
That goes whistling at the plough,
To join a merry core like this
I'm willing, aye and true.
I'll drink to them that use it
And never abuse it,
And use it aye in time,
And never fear a horse's looks
Nor yet a lassie's wime.

Some of the toasts were very bawdy:

There's to the girl with rolling eyes
The nut-brown hair between her thighs
He who the girl can't despise
God fuck and damn his bloody eyes
And may his pencil never rise
The Bugger!

There to youth and younity time
And opportunity,
a dark room,
a Feather bed,
a bonnie lass wi' her
Maiden head.

There's to the horse and the horseman's Bairns,
there's to them that lies in his airms
May the divil rock the cradle
And they to watch the horseman's Weel
or that does not wish the horseman weels.

Not unnaturally, the toasts usually return to the main theme
– drink and fellowship:

Behold and see what I will do
I will not pour this in my shoe
Nor will I drink this drink in vain
But I will drink to you again
These were all brave horses now
And then and everyone could stand His ground
and this is what I
Call a horseman's round.

The final toast of the evening was almost always to the man
who caught the first horse, Juble Cain, but it might just have
been the following:

There's to the horseman everywhere
Who keeps the secret at his heart
And who is always ready to take
A brother's part.

Hundreds of toasts have doubtless been lost due to the secrecy of the Horsemen's Society. Many were probably variations of those I have now recorded. They were all part of an elaborate ritual which new members had to memorise. If, as has been said, young ploughmen had to learn to recite the Bible backwards, then memorising the toasts would have been relatively easy in comparison.

Unlike toasts, which were only used at Society meetings when members only were present, bothy ballads [folk songs] were sung by Horsemen and non-members alike in bothies and farm kitchens, in pubs at feeing markets and at harvest home suppers. The men who sang them were often called corn kisters. They got this name because they would sit on their corn or meal kists and keep time to the music with their great hobnailed boots. Music was played on the fiddle, melodeon, accordion, mouth organ and hurdy-gurdy. Many of the songs were scurrilous with obscene words often directed at bad employers. These naturally enough never got into print except perhaps written in pencil on the back of the barn door!

Life for many men revolved around the feeing markets where farmers sought new employees and ploughmen new positions. These were important occasions for both, as a farmer could not work his farm without men and men needed work. In a non-welfare state if you didn't work, very rapidly you and your family would be reduced to begging and starvation.

Many ballads reflect the resentment felt by a ploughman towards a master who made many promises at the feeing fair and broke them as soon as the bargain was struck. The ballad *The Weary Farmers* relates a common story:

They'll tip you on the shoulder
And speir gin ye're to fee:
And they'll tell ye a fine story.
That's every word a lee;

They'll tak ye to an alehouse
And gie ye some sma' beer:
And they'll tak a drap unto themsel's
Till they get better cheer.

And when the bargain's ended
They'll toll ye out twa shillin's
And grunt and say the siller's scarce
The set o' leein villains.

Wi' cauld kail and tatties,
They feed ye up like pigs,
While they sit at their tea and toast,
Or ride into their gigs.

The chief cause of complaint on many farms was without doubt the food, as the last verse in the above ballad makes clear.

Here is another:

The breid was thick, the brose was thin,
The broth they were like bree;
I chased the barley roun' the plate,
And a' I got were three.

When plenty of work was available, a ploughman could afford to be choosy about where he worked. Bad employers had to travel to another district where no one knew their reputation for meanness to engage a ploughman:

But they'll gang on some twenty miles,
Where people disna ken them,
An there they'll fee their harvest hands,
An ae bring them far frae hame.

Ballad singers had a word of warning about bad farmers:

He'll tell ye a fine story,
Sae little ye'll hae to dae,
An' he'll ca' in the other gill
Get you for little fee;
An' he'll ca' in the other gill
Until he gets you fu,
But gin ye gang to Swaggers,
Sae sune's he'll gar ye rue.

The other common cause for complaint was the poor quality of the horses supplied. A ploughman took pride in his pair, and if they were not up to standard it was seen as a reflection on him and a good reason to move on at the next term time:

He promised me the ae best pair
That ever I clapt e'en upon;
When I went home to Barnyards,
There was naething there but skin and bone.

Another ballad was even more to the point:

We did drive on his horses,
Til they were out o' breath,
They were fitter for the tannerie,
Than for to be in graith
For want o' corn they did lie hard,
And he with us did chide,
And swore we had neglected them
Upon sweet Bogieside.

Love and lassies were never far from a young man's thoughts, and having the Word gave a ploughman a head start over other tradesmen when it came to courting. Most ploughmen certainly thought they were a cut above other country people:

The mason he's a laddie that's proud of his post,
Gin it werena for the mason we wad a' dee wi' frost,
But the mason's like the rest he'd get little for to do,
Gin it werena for the bonnie lad that handles the plough.

The tailor he's a laddie that sews at a cloot,
He'll tak' an auld coat an' he'll turn't inside out,
He'll turn't inside out, and mak' it look like new,
But he's far frae like the bonnie lad that handles the plough.

There is little doubt the local lassies tended to agree with the sentiments in the above ballad:

The tailor he's been seekin' me,
The sailor's seekin' me:
But I think I'll tak' my ploughman lad
And lat the rest gang free,
For what can a poor tailor do
When he want's candle light?
The ploughman can water his two bonnie steeds
Any hour in a' the night.

Love might be found anywhere – in a farmyard, in a field or even in a church:

When I go to the kirk on Sunday,
Mony a bonnie lass I see,
Prim, sitting by her daddy's side,
And winking o'er the pews at me.

A ploughman might have to be careful that he did not upset a jealous farmer's wife or daughter by preferring the kitchen maid:

One night into the stable,
By tryst I met her there,
On purpose for to have some fun,
And guid advice to gie her;
Our master hearing o' the same,
To the stable he cam' o'er;
And he did give us both our leave
Out o' the stable door.

But it's not upon the master
That I lay all the blame,
It is the maiden o' the place, [maiden is the eldest daughter]
That high respected dame.
Since no sweetheart to her did come,
It grieved her sore to see
The happy moments that were spent
Between my love and me.

For sweethearts who found love, the only answer was marriage – there was no living together in those days. Marriage to
a good woman for a hard-working man used to living in a
bothy with only men for company meant new responsibilities of
a wife and children, but it did have its compensations:

When my ploughman lad comes home at e'en,
He's aften wet and weary;
Cast aff the wet, put on the dry,
Come to your bed, my dearie.

I will wash my ploughman's hose,
And I will brush his o'erlay;
I will mak' my ploughman's bed,
And cheer him late and early.

Together with feeing markets and courting the lassies,
ploughing matches were important in the Horseman's calendar.
There was intense rivalry between men from different farms and
districts and much grumbling if the luck of the draw meant one
man had a less favourable part of the field to plough than a
rival:

Then some wi' pins and some wi' props,
They a' began a feein'.
Some o' them seemed to be well pleased;
And some began a – swearin'.
Some said their rigs were fearfu' teuch [tough]
Some said that theirs were stony,
The furs wad neither cut nor grip,
Nor yet look square or bonnie.

Ploughing matches were great social occasions and many had a specific purpose. When my great-grandfather took on his farm and his neighbours came to help him to catch up with the ploughing that had not been done by the previous tenant, farmers and ploughmen came from far and wide and a poem was written about the event. It was called *A Day's Darg* – a day's work:

O had ye been on Quothquan Law
On March the twenty sixth
That was the day best fittin' a'
The ploughin' match was fiz't
The men were blithe an looket weel,
Smart, healthy, everyman,
They show'd hoo neighbour farmers feel
Tae the blacksmith o' Quothquan.

For Peter is a favourite
In a' the countryside;
He shoes a horse baith weel and tight
His work was aye his pride;
The Mill and Smiddy Parks could not
Noo fit his bigger plan;
So Arthurshiels Farm he has got,
The blacksmith o' Quothquan.

Nae less than twenty nine ploughs cam'
That dae to help him on,
Wi' ploughin' his big stretch o' lan'
Before the darg was gone.
A Days Darg is a work o' love
Shows guid will man to man,
It's like tae something frae above,
Tae the blacksmith o' Quothquan.

E're gloamin grey the wark was dune
An' weel dune, judges said;
As muckle dune sae smart an sune,
An' yet nae bouncing made;
But Peter and his better half
Were kind tae horse an' man;
For mair was spread than they took aff
Bye the blacksmith o' Quothquan.

An noo tae wind this jingle up
We frankly would declare
Love Dargs should hae a wider grup;
Good deeds are far owre rare;
Good will can show in many things,
Besides the ploughin' la'
It's ain reward it always brings
As weel as at Quothquan.

This verse was written by WA Cowan, a friend of my great-grandfather, and typifies a time when neighbours helped each other and ploughmen turned out for a ploughing competition.

Many Horsemen died young as a result of the harsh conditions they were forced to endure. Tuberculosis was rife due to the damp foetid conditions encountered in many bothies. This extract is from a song written by RH Calder and was one of the most popular ballads of its day:

The Dying Ploughboy

The gloamin' winds are blawin' saft
Aroun' my lonely stable laft;
Amid the skylight's dusky red,
The sunbeams wander roun' my bed.

The doctor left me in good cheer,
But something tells me death is near;
My time on earth has nae been lang,
My time has come and I must gang.

But something in my breist gaed wrang,
A vessel burst and blood it sprang;
And as the sun sets in the skies,
They'll lay me down nae mair to rise.

Fareweel my horse, my bonnie pair,
I'll yoke and loose wi' you nae mair;
Fareweel my plough, wi' you this han'
Will turn ower nae mair fresh lan'

'Tis weel my maker knows my name,
Will he gae me a welcome hame?
As I should help in need afford,
Receive me in thy mercy, Lord.

Life could be brutally short two hundred years ago, so not surprisingly Horsemen took what pleasure they could whenever possible. If that meant sometimes an excess of drink, it is not to be wondered at:

I can drink and not be drunk,
I can fight and not be slain;
I can court another's lass,
And aye be welcome to my ain.

This was an uncompromising, boastful, tough creed which Horsemen, even if they did not quite live up to the ballad, did their best to follow.

The ballads and toasts accurately portray the life and times of the working folk of the countryside and give an insight into how they lived and their general philosophy on life, in particular the Horsemen of the Secret Society – the whisperers – who were a vital part of the farming community.

CHAPTER TWELVE

Horse Whisperers – Then and Now

MODERN HORSE WHISPERERS or equine behaviourists, to use an up-to-date term, are a very different breed from the original horse whisperers.

For a start, many present-day whisperers are female, reflecting the fact that in today's world women are much more involved than men in the day-to-day care of the modern horse which is now predominantly used for recreational purposes. As the oaths prove, women were specifically excluded from membership and from having any knowledge of the workings of the Secret Society of Horsemen. Until the beginning of last century, horse breaking and training was believed to be best left to men only.

There were some exceptions to this general rule, notably a French lady called Mademoiselle Isabel who was invited to England during the Crimean War to train cavalry horses. As may be imagined, this was frowned upon by traditional elements in the Army and her visit, despite her reputation in France, was not a great success.

In a male-dominated culture such as existed in the fermtouns of Buchan or in the rural villages of East Anglia, all the ploughmen would have agreed with the folklore that the presence of a woman could in some way taint and weaken a horse, especially during the training process. Such thinking now seems archaic, as it is generally recognised that women are often more talented horse trainers than men. Their quieter and gentler approach to handling horses is now accepted as most likely to meet with the greatest success.

Modern whisperers use different techniques to the original whisperers and their methods are based on their understanding of horse psychology as first expounded by the American Monty Roberts. He developed his techniques from his observations of wild horses and how the leading or dominant mare controlled and disciplined the herd. Monty Roberts had been revolted by the traditional way employed by his father to break wild horses. This exposed the horse that was being broken to every situation that would cause it fear and alarm until these became so commonplace that they were accepted by the animal.

The wild horse would be made to run down a narrow race and then crushed tightly enough to allow a head collar to be placed on it. A rope was attached to the head collar and tied to a solid post. The animal, on release from the crush, would fight against this restraint, which was made all the more difficult for it as the rope was fixed about six feet up the post. Once the horse had quietened down, the breaker would stand back in the corral with a heavy tarpaulin or weighted sack which he threw over the animal's back. It is easy to imagine the panic this caused the horse and many were so terrified that they fought the restraint of the rope to the point where they injured themselves. This process could continue for up to four days.

The next stage was to tie up each leg in turn. This was done by attaching a rope around the pastern which is that part of the leg below the fetlock. The end of the rope was then pulled up through a neck collar and the sacking would be repeated. The process with the legs would take up to ten days and the animal would be severely traumatised and often damaged, with rope burns at the very least. This was all done with the express purpose of breaking the horse's spirit, or as old Horsemen in the Cambridgeshire Fens would say, 'breaking its heart'.

Once the animal was totally subdued, it was harnessed or saddled and ridden. If it fought, it would be subdued again and whipped until it gave in. The whole process was a horrible procedure which could take weeks, and it was hardly surprising that the young Monty Roberts wanted nothing to do with the method and was determined to find a kinder approach. This he did, and he reckoned he could subdue even the wildest animal in three to four hours without any cruelty.

He spent many months on the American prairie observing wild mustangs and their herd behaviour. He saw very quickly that the dominant mare, the matriarch of the herd, dominated the rest of the animals – even unruly youngsters – by using body language and eye contact. He realised that the horse being a herd animal is not comfortable by itself. It wants and needs companionship.

He watched how the matriarchal mare would discipline a badly behaved colt. First she would kick him hard and then drive him out of the herd and keep him out by watching him all the time – keeping him out alone. He would be terrified to be left on his own and eventually make submissive movements to the mare. She wouldn't give in. She would keep her eye on him with her body square on to him. He would make mouth movements of licking and chewing which is a submissive gesture meaning 'I am no threat to you'. The alpha stallion would be quite unconcerned with this procedure, only interested in protecting his herd from other stallions who might want to poach some of the females or even take over the entire herd.

The mare would eventually relent and allow the colt back into the group and start to groom him with her teeth. She would groom the neck, then back and then hindquarters, and when this process was finished he would be back in the herd. If over the next few days or weeks, he behaved badly again, the mare would repeat the process, driving him out and then allowing him back when he submitted.

By watching the wild mustangs, Roberts learned the equine body language. The key ingredient of the language, which he came to call Equus, is the positioning of the body and its direction of travel. He believed that the attitude of the horse's body relative to the long axis of the spine is critical to how it communicates. To drive the colt away, the mare would look at the colt directly, spine rigid and head pointing directly at him. The colt would have to stay 200 to 300 metres away from the herd. After a period of isolation and once the animal had indicated by submissive movements that he was truly penitent, the mare would turn her long axis to the animal and stop eye contact. In simple terms, if the mare was sideways on to him, the colt was allowed to rejoin the herd. Signs of submission and penitence include not just lip and mouth movements but walking backwards and forwards with the nose close to the ground.

Roberts based his technique of horse whispering on these observations. He believed that to push the young horse away from you by direct eye contact and aggressive body movements would instinctively make it want to return. Once the animal gives the signal by mouth movements and lowering its head of wanting to submit, the whisperer then changes his or her body conformation and ceases to be confrontational. This in simple terms usually just means turning sideways on to the horse and dropping eye contact. Roberts called this 'advance and retreat'. He used the horse's own language and system of communication to create a relationship between the animal and the man. Over the years he refined the technique which he came to call 'Joined-Up. 'Join-Up' occurs when man and horse are finally in harmony and the horse trusts the man (or woman) to saddle and finally ride it.

The Join-Up technique can also be demonstrated with cattle. If you walk through a field of cows and make direct eye contact with them, their reaction is to run away. If you turn your back on them, they will advance and come right up to you and even touch you. I always thought this was simple curiosity, but perhaps Roberts is right and it is all part of herd instinct and herd discipline. Cattle too are herbivores and herd animals and subject in the wild to predation just like horses. It would be interesting to see a good modern horse whisperer work with a wild cow and observe the outcome. However, it's not a scenario that is likely to happen, for modern horse whisperers have the same contempt for cattle work as their original counterparts.

Roberts and the many advocates of his method say that it will work for anyone who has a knowledge of horses, is calm and is prepared to be patient, willing to listen and be observant.

Roberts summed up his successful technique as having three cardinal rules. Firstly, the worst piece of horsemanship is to intentionally cause the animal pain. Most of the original whisperers would have agreed with this, as it was a specific part of their Secret Oath not to allow a horse to be 'badly used' which obliged them also to prevent any one else from physically harming a horse.

Roberts' second rule was never to use a single line-lunge. He believed this time-honoured method of training horses to get them used to voice commands can cause untold damage to the neck and spine. As a veterinary surgeon working with horses over 30 years, I find this difficult to agree with. Everyone in modern times is taught how to lunge a horse and is aware of the positive advantages to be gained by using the method. Lunging heavy horses was not a technique used by many of the old whisperers but I doubt they would have thought it harmful.

Roberts' last rule is one that runs completely counter to the old whisperers' techniques – never feed a horse from the hand. There is no doubt that done indiscriminately it can cause many animals to be 'nippy' and turn them into biters, but for the original horse whisperers it was part and parcel of their method to control and encourage their plough horses. The old horse whisperers' and the modern whisperers' methods are therefore very different.

Skilled patient people with an intuitive understanding of horses will often work what seem to ignorant outsiders to be miracles with difficult animals. In the last ten years, Roberts' techniques have been followed and used with varying success. Some people are frankly poor advocates for his system, and I have had experience of this.

One of my clients had two wild Exmoor ponies which she had rescued off the moor. They were run into loose boxes and she expected that, given a few days of peace and quiet and some feed, they would settle down and allow themselves to be handled. Three months later they could still not be caught and she called in a horse whisperer. I saw the lady in action. She was making exaggerated yawning gestures and strange ballet like movements with her hands and arms. This went on for some hours, but the animals remained unimpressed and uncaught. In the end I had to resort to feeding them some tranquilliser and I then caught them with a lasso. They soon settled down and have turned into two happy willing ponies. I couldn't help thinking at the time that an original horse whisperer would have gone into the loose box, shut the door and had them both caught and eating out of his hand in a very short space of time.

Although old and new horse whisperers differ fundamentally in their techniques and methods of handling horses, many things unite the old ploughmen, who were the first to be called whisperers due to their habit of standing on the near side of the horse with one hand on its muzzle and whispering the Word in the animal's ear, and present-day exponents of the Monty Roberts school of horse whispering. Old and new share a regard and love for their animals and respect them.

Cynics might suggest that the old whisperers deliberately misled a gullible public by pretending that a magic Word was the secret of their success in handling horses. The same cynics might think there may be more behind modern Whispering techniques than is superficially apparent. Eye contact and hypnotism may be far more important to modern whispering than acting out a primitive herd ritual. Some Whisperers are very skilled and produce amazing results, while others are better at talking than taming.

Postscript

AS FARMING BECAME MORE mechanised, fewer people were required to work the land. This led to an inevitable drift from the countryside to the towns where work could be obtained in the new factories created by the burgeoning Industrial Revolution. People left the land in droves. They might have preferred to stay but there was little choice. It was move or starve. Many became economic migrants to Australia, New Zealand, Canada and the USA, and among them were horse whisperers who took their methods and secrets with them. Their descendants retain folk memories and plenty of them have written to me telling stories of grandfathers and great-grandfathers who had an uncanny knack of handling horses.

Secret Societies have many common links and influences which are, by their nature, very difficult to prove. The Confederate Army in the Southern States are said to have recruited Scottish Whisperers specifically because of their reputed expertise with handling horses.

Little known is the fact that after the American Civil War, between Christmas 1865 and June 1866, six young Confederate cavalry officers of Scottish descent, bored with having nothing to do, formed a hell-raising secret society, which they called the Ku Klux Klan. The idea for the name came from the Greek *kuklos*, meaning a circle, which was altered to 'kuklux', as this sounded better and no-one knew what it meant. 'Klan' was added, as it seemed to follow on from their Scottish background.

These men were James Crowe, Richard Reed, Calvin Jones, John Lester, Frank McCord and John Kennedy. They were all well educated. Four were budding lawyers; McCord became the editor of a local paper, and Lester a politician.

Non-members who wanted to join the Klan were picked up unexpectedly in the evening, blindfolded and taken to a remote barn where they were put through a quasi-religious initiation ceremony before an altar. All initiates of the KKK had to take an oath in which they solemnly swore never to reveal any of the secrets, symbols, signs, grips, passwords, mysteries or purpose of the KKK. Once this oath was taken, the new member also had to swear that he would never reveal anything that he might learn about the Klan that night, so help him God.

The Ku Klux Klan rapidly took on a more sinister aspect when it became a white supremacist society, rapidly forgetting its origins as it spread over the Southern States of America like wildfire, fuelled by hatred and fear of the black population of that land.

As far as I can discover, the Secret Society of Horsemen did not spread to Europe, although there is plenty of evidence that the gypsies, or Romanies, throughout the continent had special skills, secrets and 'cures' not dissimilar to those used by the original whisperers. They too claimed to tame horses by whispering secret words in the animal's ear.

Other cultures in other continents also seemed to have traditions of 'whispering' to horses, which have no obvious links to the Scottish Secret Societies. North American Indians used to chew herbs and plants, then blow up the nose of the horse to calm it down. Gauchos in South America did something similar with tobacco. They would chew a wad, then spit the liquid or blow the tobacco smell up the horse's nostril. This was said by some to be the origin of the term 'horse whisperer', as onlookers would see just what they would have in Scotland; a man apparently whispering to an animal, which immediately changed from being nervous and upset to being calm and biddable.

There is little doubt that the methods used by the original horse whisperers, using different smells to influence the behaviour of their horses, could be used to great effect today. The average horse owner could develop the techniques that the old whisperers used to the great benefit of both horse and handler. Even in the highly charged horseracing world, the use of aromatic spices such as rosemary, cinnamon or fennel would do much to calm an excitable or neurotic thoroughbred and make it easier and more compliant to handle. It's aromatherapy for horses and it does work! Using smells to control horses in a modern world could also have a downside, however. The outcome of any equine competitive event such as horseracing or jumping could be influenced one way or another by conditioning an animal to react to a jading or hexing smell, which caused it to stop or refuse a fence or goad it on to greater effort. It would only take a knowledgeable individual leaning over a railing with a noxious (to the horse) smell emanating from his or her person, undetected by human nostrils to influence the outcome of a competition. It may have already happened for all I am aware. Who knows? It's an intriguing thought.

By gathering together the different strands from many different sources and people who have been kind enough to help me in my quest, I hope I have gone some way towards keeping alive memories of the original horse whisperers and ensuring that their legacy will be remembered forever.

Bibliography

Adams, David G, *Bothy Nichts and Days*
Beery, Jesse, *How to Break and Train Horses*
Cameron, David Kerr, *The Ballad and the Plough*
Cameron, David Kerr, *The Cornkister Days*
Carter, Ian, *Farm Life in North East Scotland 1840 – 1914*
Devine, TM, *Farm Servants and Labour in Lowland Scotland*
Evans, George Ewart, *Ask the Fellows Who Cut the Hay*
Evans, George Ewart, *Horse Power and Magic*
Evans, George Ewart, *Pattern Under the Plough*
Fenton, Alexander, *Scottish Country Life*
Fraser, Andrew, *The Native Horses of Scotland*
Hole, Christina, *English Folklore*
James, Simon, *The Atlantic Celts*
Jones, Evan John, *The Secrets of Horse Whispering*
Kennung, *I Plooman's Greps an Werd*
Nimmo, William P, *The Art of Horsemanship*
Porteous, Tom, *A Living from the Land*
Richardson, Clive, *The Horse Breakers*
Smout, TC, *A Century of the Scottish People*
Sprott, Gavin, *Scotland's Past in Action – Farming*
Stephen, Henry, *Book of the Farm*
Symon, JA, *Scottish Farming Past and Present*

The Scottish Farmer
The Scots Magazine

Some other books published by **LUATH** PRESS

Men & Beasts: Wild Men and Tame Animals of Scotland

Poems and Prose by Valerie Gillies
Photographs by Rebecca Marr
ISBN 0 946487 92 8 PB £15.00

 Come and meet some wild men and tame beasts. Explore the fleeting moment and capture the passing of time in these portrait studies which document a year's journey. Travel across Scotland with poet Valerie Gillies and photographer Rebecca Marr: share their passion for a land where wild men can sometimes be tamed and tame beasts can get really wild.

Among the wild men they find are a gunner in Edinburgh Castle, a Highland shepherd, a ferryman on the River Almond, an eel fisher on Loch Ness, a Borders fencer, and a beekeeper on a Lowland estate.

The beasts portrayed in their own settings include Clydesdale foals, Scottish deerhounds, Highland cattle, blackface sheep, falcons, lurchers, bees, pigs, cashmere goats, hens, cockerels, tame swans and transgenic lambs.

Photograph, poem and reportage – a unique take on Scotland today.

'Goin aroon the Borders wi Valerie an' Rebecca did my reputation the world o good. It's no often they see us wi beautiful talented women, ye ken.' WALTER ELLIOT, fencer and historian

'These poems are rooted in the elemental world.' ROBERT NYE, reviewing The Chanter's Tune in The Times

'Valerie Gillies is one of the most original voices of the fertile avant-guarde Scottish poetry.' MARCO FAZZINI, l'Arco, Italia

'The work of Valerie Gillies and Rebecca Marr is the result of true collaboration based on insight, empathy and generosity.' JULIE LAWSON, Studies in Photography

'Rebecca Marr's photos never fall into the trap of mere illustration, but rather they show a very individual vision – creative interpretation rather than prosaic document.' ROBIN GILLANDERS, photographer

Half the royalties genereated from the sale of this publication will go to Maggie's Centre for the care of cancer patients.

THE QUEST FOR

The Quest for the Nine Maidens

Stuart McHardy
ISBN 0 946487 66 9 HB £16.99

 When Arthur was conveyed to Avalon they were there. When Odin summoned warriors to Valhalla they were there. When the Greek god Apollo was worshipped on mountaintops they were there. When Brendan came to the Island of Women they there. Cerridwen's cauldron of inspiration was tended by them and Peredur received his arms from them. They are found in Pictland, Wales, Ireland, Iceland, Gaul, Greece, Africa and possibly as far as field as South America and Oceania.

They are the Nine Maidens, pagan priestesses involved in the worship of the Mother Goddess. From Stone Age rituals to the 20th century, the Nine Maidens come in many forms. Muses, Maenads, valkyries and druidesses all associated with a single male. Weather - workers, shape - shifters, diviners and healers, the Nine Maidens are linked to the Old Religion over much of our planet. In this book Stuart McHardy has traced similar groups of Nine Maidens, throughout the ancient Celtic and Germanic world and far beyond, from Christian and pagan sources. In his search he begins to uncover one of the most ancient and widespread institutions of human society.

The Quest for Arthur

Stuart McHardy
ISBN 1 84282 012 5 HB £16.99

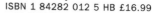 King Arthur of Camelot and the Knights of the Round Table are enduring romantic figures. A national hero for the Bretons, the Welsh and the English alike Arthur is a potent figure for many. This quest leads to a radical new interpretation of the ancient myth.

Historian, storyteller and folklorist Stuart McHardy believes he has uncovered the origins of this inspirational figure, the true Arthur. He incorporates knowledge of folklore and placename studies with an archaeological understanding of the 6th century.

Combining knowledge of the earliest records and histories of Arthur with an awareness of the importance of oral traditions, this quest leads to the discovery that the enigmatic origins of Arthur lie not in Brittany or England or Wales. Instead they lie in that magic land the ancient Welsh called Y Gogledd, the North; the North of Britain which we now call Scotland.

The Quest for the Celtic Key

Karen Ralls-MacLeod and
Ian Robertson
ISBN 0 946487 73 1 HB £18.99

Who were the Picts? The Druids? The Celtic saints?

Was the famous 'murdered Apprentice' carving at Rosslyn Chapel deliberately altered in the past? If so, why?

Why has Rossslyn Chapel been a worldwide mecca for churchmen, Freemasons, Knights Templar, and Rosicrucians?

Why are there so many Scottish connections to King Arthur and Merlin?

What was the famous 'Blue Blanket' of the medieval Guilds of Edinburgh?

Did Prince Henry Sinclair get to North America before Columbus?

'The reader who travels with Karen Ralls-MacLeod and Ian Robertson...will find a travelogue which enriches the mythologies and histories so beautifully told, with many newly wrought connections to places, buildings, stones and other remains which may still be viewed in the landscape and historic monuments of modern Scotland....'

Rev. Dr. Michael Northcott, FACULTY OF DIVINITY, UNIVERSITY OF EDINBURGH

'Karen Ralls-MacLeod is endowed with that rare jewel of academia: a sharp and inquisitive mind blessed with a refreshing openness. Her stimulating work has the gift of making the academic accessible, and brings a clear and sound basis to the experiential... from

'Idylls of the King' to 'Indiana Jones', the search for the Holy Grail will never be the same again. This is a 'must read' book for all who sense the mystery and magic of our distant past.'

Robert Bauval, BESTSELLING AUTHOR OF 'THE SECRET CHAMBER', and 'KEEPER OF GENESIS'

WILD LIVES

Foxes: the Blood is Wild

Bridget MacCaskill
ISBN 0 946487 71 5 PBK £9.99
A 'must' for those who respect and care for foxes!

WILDLIFE GUARDIAN

In the endless struggle between man and nature, Bridget and Don MacCaskill's Highland home has always been a haven for injured and orphaned wildlife, from red deer to wildcats. The fascinating story begins with the rescue of two near-starved fox cubs called Rufus and Rusty, victims of their species' vicious reputation, and charts their often amusing journey into adulthood under the watchful eye of their new human 'parents'. Along the way, they are regularly joined by other wild creatures in need of the MacCaskills' help – badgers, birds of prey and a majestic golden eagle among them.

The Blood is Wild is a dramatic yet touching, brilliantly observed account of the precarious existence of wildlife in the Highlands. It is written with the same fondness that was so infectious in the TV film and book *On the Swirl of the Tide*, the story about the survival of otters in the North of Scotland.

Their book has suspense, marvellous scenery and practical information... good armchair reading and more. Don's photographs are superb.

NAOMI LEWIS, EVENING STANDARD

The Blood is Wild is funny and moving... This wildlife epic will bring much joy to animal lovers. TODAY

Otters: On the Swirl of the Tide

Bridget MacCaskill

ISBN 0 946487 67 7 PBK £9.99

Otters have a strong appeal and deserve all the books they can get. No wonder the MacCaskills were enchanted. Nicholas Wollaston,

OBSERVER

The story of Bodach, Palethroat and Pinknose unfolded to Bridget and Don MacCaskill over a period of twelve patient years. Slowly, the wild otters became accustomed to the scent of the humans around their remote Highland sea loch, and the couple were able to observe the habits and behaviour of these beautiful creatures. Cubs are born and grow up with their parents, and the otters regularly encounter other animals, sometimes with amusing results. Whatever the event, Bridget and Don are there with pen and camera, ready to record the details.

On the Swirl of the Tide is a vivid and intimate portrait of the lives of otters in the wild, part of which was shared with the cameras for Central Television's Nature Watch series. The beautiful colour photographs from Don MacCaskill reveal details never before shown, and Bridget's sympathetic portrait of the lifestyle and behaviour of these wild creatures is the most enchanting and powerful account of otter life since Gavin Maxwell's bestseller *A Ring of Bright Water*. Whereas Maxwell's wonderful account primarily focuses on otters in a domestic setting, the otters in this book are truly wild.

A marvellous tale of adventures with otters... there is much beauty in the book.

EVERGREEN

Superb photographs. The opportunities to observe and photograph their feeding, grooming play, and mating in full daylight were unique.

ALAN BENNETT, DAILY TELEGRAPH

This book is sure to leave everybody wanting a second helping.

JOHN CRICHTON, SCOTTISH WILDLIFE

NATURAL SCOTLAND

Listen to the Trees

Don MacCaskill

ISBN 0 946487 65 0 PBK £9.99

Don MacCaskill is one of Scotland's foremost naturalists, conservationists and wildlife photographers. *Listen to the Trees* is a beautiful and acutely observed account of how his outlook on life began to change as trees, woods, forests and all the wonders that they contain became a focus in his life. It is rich in its portrayal of the life that moves in the Caledonian forest and on the moorlands – lofty twig-stacked heronries, the elusive peregrine falcon and the red, bushy-tailed fox – of the beauty of the trees, and of those who worked in the forests.

'Trees are surely the supreme example of a life-force stronger than our own,' writes Don MacCaskill. 'Some, like the giant redwoods of North America, live for thousands of years. Some, like our own oaks and pines, may live for centuries. All, given the right conditions, will regenerate their species and survive long into the future.'

In the afterword Dr Philip Ratcliffe, former Head of the Forestry Commission's Environment Branch and a leading environment consultant, discusses the future role of Britain's forests – their influence on the natural environment and on the communities that live and work in and around them.

'Listen to the Trees will inspire all those with an interest in nature. It is a beautiful account, strongly anecdotal and filled with humour.'

RENNIE McOWAN

'This man adores trees. 200 years from now, your descendants will know why.'

JIM GILCHRIST, THE SCOTSMAN

Red Sky at Night

John Barrington

ISBN 0 946487 60 X PBK £8.99

'I read John Barrington's book with growing delight. This working shepherd writes beautifully about his animals, about the wildlife, trees and flowers which surround him at all

times, and he paints an unforgettable picture of his glorious corner of Western Scotland. It is a lovely story of a rather wonderful life'. JAMES HERRIOT

John Barrington is a shepherd to over 750 Blackface ewes who graze 2,000 acres of some of Britain's most beautiful hills overlooking the deep dark water of Loch Katrine in Perthshire. The yearly round of lambing, dipping, shearing and the sales is marvellously interwoven into the story of the glen, of Rob Roy in whose house John now lives, of curling when the ice is thick enough, and of sheep dog trials in the summer. Whether up to the hills or along the glen, John knows the haunts of the local wildlife: the wily hill fox, the grunting badger, the herds of red deer, and the shrews, voles and insects which scurry underfoot. He sets his seasonal clock by the passage of birds on the loch, and jealously guards over the golden eagle's eyrie in the hills. Paul Armstrong's sensitive illustrations are the perfect accompaniment to the evocative text.

'Mr Barrington is a great pleasure to read. One learns more things about the countryside from this account of one year than from a decade of The Archers'. THE DAILY TELEGRAPH

'Powerful and evocative... a book which brings vividly to life the landscape, the wildlife, the farm animals and the people who inhabit John's vista. He makes it easy for the reader to fall in love with both his surrounds and his commune with nature'. THE SCOTTISH FIELD

'An excellent and informative book.... not only an account of a shepherd's year but also the diary of a naturalist. Little escapes Barrington's enquiring eye and, besides the life cycle of a sheep, he also gives those of every bird, beast, insect and plant that crosses his path, mixing their histories with descriptions of the geography, local history and folklore of his surroundings'. TLS

'The family life at Glengyle is wholesome, appealing and not without a touch of the Good Life. Many will envy Mr Barrington his fastness home as they cruise up Loch Katrine on the tourist steamer'. THE FIELD

Wild Scotland: The essential guide to finding the best of natural Scotland

James McCarthy

Photography by Laurie Campbell

ISBN 0 946487 37 5 PBK £8.99

With a foreword by Magnus Magnusson and striking colour photographs by Laurie Campbell, this is the essential up-to-date guide to viewing wildlife in Scotland for the visitor and resident alike. It provides a fascinating overview of the country's plants, animals, bird and marine life against the background of their typical natural settings, as an introduction to the vivid descriptions of the most accessible localities, linked to clear regional maps. A unique feature is the focus on 'green tourism' and sustainable visitor use of the countryside, contributed by Duncan Bryden, manager of the Scottish Tourist Board's Tourism and the Environment Task Force. Important practical information on access and the best times of year for viewing sites makes this an indispensable and user-friendly travelling companion to anyone interested in exploring Scotland's remarkable natural heritage.

James McCarthy is former Deputy Director for Scotland of the Nature Conservancy Council, and now a Board Member of Scottish Natural Heritage and Chairman of the Environmental Youth Work National Development Project Scotland.

Scotland, Land and People: An Inhabited Solitude:

James McCarthy

ISBN 0 946487 57 X PBK £7.99

'Scotland is the country above all others that I have seen, in which a man of imagination may carve out his own pleasures; there are so many inhabited solitudes.'

DOROTHY WORDSWORTH, in her journal of August 1803

An informed and thought-provoking profile of Scotland's unique landscapes and the impact of humans on what we see now and in the future. James McCarthy leads us through the many aspects of the land and the people who inhabit it: natural Scotland; the rocks beneath; land ownership; the use of resources; people and place; conserving Scotland's heritage and much more.

Written in a highly readable style, this concise volume offers an understanding of the land as a whole. Emphasising the uniqueness of the Scottish environment, the author explores the links between this and other aspects of our culture as a key element in rediscovering a modern sense of the Scottish identity and perception of nationhood.

'This book provides an engaging introduction to the mysteries of Scotland's people and landscapes. Difficult concepts are described in simple terms, providing the interested Scot or tourist with an invaluable overview of the country... It fills an important niche which, to my knowledge, is filled by no other publications.'
BETSY KING, Chief Executive, Scottish Environmental Education Council.

The Highland Geology Trail
John L Roberts

ISBN 0 946487 36 7 PBK £4.99

Where can you find the oldest rocks in Europe?
Where can you see ancient hills around 800 million years old?
How do you tell whether a valley was carved out by a glacier, not a river?
What are the Fucoid Beds?
Where do you find rocks folded like putty?
How did great masses of rock pile up like snow in front of a snow-plough?
When did volcanoes spew lava and ash to form Skye, Mull and Rum?
Where can you find fossils on Skye?

'...a lucid introduction to the geological record in general, a jargon-free exposition of the regional background, and a series of descriptions of specific localities of geological interest on a "trail" around the highlands.
Having checked out the local references on the ground, I can vouch for their accuracy and look forward to investigating farther afield, informed by this guide.
Great care has been taken to explain specific terms as they occur and, in so doing, John Roberts has created a resource of great value which is eminently usable by anyone with an

interest in the outdoors...the best bargain you are likely to get as a geology book in the foreseeable future.'
Jim Johnston, PRESS AND JOURNAL

Rum: Nature's Island
Magnus Magnusson

ISBN 0 946487 32 4 PBK £7.95

Rum: Nature's Island is the fascinating story of a Hebridean island from the earliest times through to the Clearances and its period as the sporting playground of a Lancashire industrial magnate, and on to its rebirth as a National Nature Reserve, a model for the active ecological management of Scotland's wild places.

Thoroughly researched and written in a lively accessible style, the book includes comprehensive coverage of the island's geology, animals and plants, and people, with a special chapter on the Edwardian extravaganza of Kinloch Castle. There is practical information for visitors to what was once known as 'the Forbidden Isle'; the book provides details of bothy and other accommodation, walks and nature trails. It closes with a positive vision for the island's future: biologically diverse, economically dynamic and ecologically sustainable.

Rum: Nature's Island is published in co-operation with Scottish Natural Heritage (of which Magnus Magnusson is Chairman) to mark the 40th anniversary of the acquisition of Rum by its predecessor, The Nature Conservancy.

ON THE TRAIL OF

On the Trail of John Muir
Cherry Good

ISBN 0 946487 62 6 PBK £7.99

Follow the man who made the US go green. Confidant of presidents, father of American National Parks, trailblazer of world conservation and voted a Man of the Millennium in the US, John Muir's life and work is of continuing relevance. A man ahead of his time who saw the wilderness he loved threatened by industrialisation and determined to protect it, a crusade in which he was largely successful. His love of the wilderness began at an early age and he was filled with wanderlust all his life.

'Only by going in silence, without baggage, can on truly get into the heart of the wilderness. All other travel is mere dust and hotels and baggage and chatter.' JOHN MUIR

Braving mosquitoes and black bears Cherry Good set herself on his trail – Dunbar, Scotland; Fountain Lake and Hickory Hill, Wisconsin; Yosemite Valley and the Sierra Nevada, California; the Grand Canyon, Arizona; Alaska; and Canada – to tell his story. John Muir was himself a prolific writer, and Good draws on his books, articles, letters and diaries to produce an account that is lively, intimate, humorous and anecdotal, and that provides refreshing new insights into the hero of world conservation.

> John Muir chronology
>
> General map plus 10 detailed maps covering the US, Canada and Scotland
>
> Original colour photographs
>
> Afterword advises on how to get involved
>
> Conservation websites and addresses

Muir's importance has long been acknowledged in the US with over 200 sites of scenic beauty named after him. He was a Founder of The Sierra Club which now has over ¹/₂ million members. Due to the movement he started some 360 million acres of wilderness are now protected. This is a book which shows Muir not simply as a hero but as likeable humorous and self-effacing man of extraordinary vision.

'I do hope that those who read this book will burn with the same enthusiasm for John Muir which the author shows.'
WEST HIGHLAND FREE PRESS

POLITICS & CURRENT ISSUES

Scotlands of the Mind
Angus Calder
ISBN 1 84282 008 7 PB £9.99

Trident on Trial: the case for people's disarmament
Angie Zelter
ISBN 1 84282 004 4 PB £9.99

Uncomfortably Numb: A Prison Requiem
Maureen Maguire
ISBN 1 84282 001 X PB £8.99

Scotland: Land & Power – Agenda for Land Reform
Andy Wightman
ISBN 0 946487 70 7 PB £5.00

Old Scotland New Scotland
Jeff Fallow
ISBN 0 946487 40 5 PB £6.99

Some Assembly Required: Scottish Parliament
David Shepherd
ISBN 0 946487 84 7 PB £7.99

Notes from the North
Emma Wood
ISBN 0 946487 46 4 PB £8.99

NATURAL WORLD

The Hydro Boys: pioneers of renewable energy
Emma Wood
ISBN 1 84282 016 8 HB £16.99

'Nothing but Heather!'
Gerry Cambridge
ISBN 0 946487 49 9 PB £15.00

ISLANDS

The Islands that Roofed the World: Easdale, Belnahua, Luing & Seil:
Mary Withall
ISBN 0 946487 76 6 PB £4.99

TRAVEL & LEISURE

Die Kleine Schottlandfibel [Scotland Guide in German]
Hans-Walter Arends
ISBN 0 946487 89 8 PB £8.99

Let's Explore Edinburgh Old Town
Anne Bruce English
ISBN 0 946487 98 7 PB £4.99

Edinburgh's Historic Mile
Duncan Priddle
ISBN 0 946487 97 9 PB £2.99

Pilgrims in the Rough: St Andrews beyond the 19th hole
Michael Tobert
ISBN 0 946487 74 X PB £7.99

FOOD & DRINK

The Whisky Muse: Scotch whisky in poem & song
various, ed. Robin Laing
ISBN 0 946487 95 2 PB £12.99

First Foods Fast: good simple baby meals
Lara Boyd
ISBN 1 84282 002 8 PB £4.99

Edinburgh and Leith Pub Guide
Stuart McHardy
ISBN 0 946487 80 4 PB £4.95

WALK WITH LUATH

Skye 360: walking the coastline of Skye
Andrew Dempster
ISBN 0 946487 85 5 PB £8.99

The Joy of Hillwalking
Ralph Storer
ISBN 0 946487 28 6 PB £7.50

Scotland's Mountains before the Mountaineers
Ian R Mitchell
ISBN 0 946487 39 1 PB £9.99

Mountain Days and Bothy Nights
Dave Brown and Ian R Mitchell
ISBN 0 946487 15 4 PB £7.50

SPORT

Ski & Snowboard Scotland
Hilary Parke
ISBN 0 946487 35 9 PB £6.99

Over the Top with the Tartan Army
Andy McArthur
ISBN 0 946487 45 6 PB £7.99

BIOGRAPHY

The Last Lighthouse
Sharma Krauskopf
ISBN 0 946487 96 0 PB £7.99

Tobermory Teuchter
Peter Macnab
ISBN 0 946487 41 3 PB £7.99

Bare Feet and Tackety Boots
Archie Cameron
ISBN 0 946487 17 0 PB £7.95

Come Dungeons Dark
John Taylor Caldwell
ISBN 0 946487 19 7 PB £6.95

HISTORY

Civil Warrior:
The Extraordinary Life and Complete Poetical Works of James Graham, First Marquis of Montrose, 1612–1650
Robin Bell
ISBN 1 84282 013 3 HB £10.99

A Passion for Scotland
David R Ross
ISBN 1 84282 019 2 PB £5.99

Reportage Scotland
Louise Yeoman
ISBN 0 946487 61 8 PB £9.99

Blind Harry's Wallace
Hamilton of Gilbertfield
introduced by Elspeth King
illustrations by Owain Kirby
ISBN 0 946487 33 2 PB £8.99

SOCIAL HISTORY

Pumpherston: the story of a shale oil village
Sybil Cavanagh
ISBN 1 84282 011 7 HB £17.99
ISBN 1 84282 015 X PB £7.99

Shale Voices
Alistair Findlay
ISBN 0 946487 78 2 HB £17.99
ISBN 0 946487 63 4 PB £10.99

A Word for Scotland
Jack Campbell
ISBN 0 946487 48 0 PB £12.99

ON THE TRAIL OF

On the Trail of William Wallace
David R Ross
ISBN 0 946487 47 2 PB £7.99

On the Trail of Robert the Bruce
David R Ross
ISBN 0 946487 52 9 PB £7.99

On the Trail of Mary Queen of Scots
J Keith Cheetham
ISBN 0 946487 50 2 PB £7.99

On the Trail of Bonnie Prince Charlie
David R Ross
ISBN 0 946487 68 5 PB £7.99

On the Trail of Robert Burns
John Cairney
ISBN 0 946487 51 0 PB £7.99

On the Trail of Queen Victoria in the Highlands
Ian R Mitchell
ISBN 0 946487 79 0 PB £7.99

On the Trail of Robert Service
G Wallace Lockhart
ISBN 0 946487 24 3 PB £7.99

On the Trail of the Pilgrim Fathers
J Keith Cheetham
ISBN 0 946487 83 9 PB £7.99

FOLKLORE

Luath Storyteller: Highland Myths & Legends
George W Macpherson
ISBN 1 84282 003 6 PB £5.00

GENEALOGY

Scottish Roots: step-by-step guide for ancestor hunters
Alwyn James
ISBN 1 84282 007 9 PB £9.99

WEDDINGS, MUSIC AND DANCE

The Scottish Wedding Book
G Wallace Lockhart
ISBN 1 94282 010 9 PB £12.99

Fiddles and Folk
G Wallace Lockhart
ISBN 0 946487 38 3 PB £7.95

Highland Balls and Village Halls
G Wallace Lockhart
ISBN 0 946487 12 X PB £6.95

POETRY

Bad Ass Raindrop
Kokumo Rocks
ISBN 1 84282 018 4 PB £6.99

Caledonian Cramboclink: the Poetry of
William Neill
ISBN 0 946487 53 7 PB £8.99

Luath Burns Companion
John Cairney
ISBN 1 84282 000 1 PB £10.00

Scots Poems to be read aloud
collected and introduced by
Stuart McHardy
ISBN 0 946487 81 2 PB £5.00

Poems to be read aloud
collected and introduced by
Tom Atkinson
ISBN 0 946487 00 6 PB £5.00

CARTOONS

Broomie Law
Cinders McLeod
ISBN 0 946487 99 5 PB £4.00

FICTION

The Road Dance
John MacKay
ISBN 1 84282 024 9 PB £9.99

Milk Treading
Nick Smith
ISBN 0 946487 75 8 PB £9.99

The Strange Case of RL Stevenson
Richard Woodhead
ISBN 0 946487 86 3 HB £16.99

But n Ben A-Go-Go
Matthew Fitt
ISBN 1 84282 014 1 PB £6.99
ISBN 0 946487 82 0 HB £10.99

The Bannockburn Years
William Scott
ISBN 0 946487 34 0 PB £7.95

The Great Melnikov
Hugh MacLachlan
ISBN 0 946487 42 1 PB £7.95

LANGUAGE

Luath Scots Language Learner [Book]
L Colin Wilson
ISBN 0 946487 91 X PB £9.99

Luath Scots Language Learner [Double Audio CD Set]
L Colin Wilson
ISBN 1 84282 026 5 CD £16.99

Luath Press Limited
committed to publishing well written books worth reading

LUATH PRESS takes its name from Robert Burns, whose little collie Luath (*Gael.*, swift or nimble) tripped up Jean Armour at a wedding and gave him the chance to speak to the woman who was to be his wife and the abiding love of his life. Burns called one of *The Twa Dogs* Luath after Cuchullin's hunting dog in *Ossian's Fingal*. Luath Press was established in 1981 in the heart of Burns country, and is now based a few steps up the road from Burns' first lodgings on Edinburgh's Royal Mile.

Luath offers you distinctive writing with a hint of unexpected pleasures.

Most bookshops in the UK, the US, Canada, Australia, New Zealand and parts of Europe either carry our books in stock or can order them for you. To order direct from us, please send a £sterling cheque, postal order, international money order or your credit card details (number, address of cardholder and expiry date) to us at the address below. Please add post and packing as follows: UK – £1.00 per delivery address; overseas surface mail – £2.50 per delivery address; overseas airmail – £3.50 for the first book to each delivery address, plus £1.00 for each additional book by airmail to the same address. If your order is a gift, we will happily enclose your card or message at no extra charge.

Luath Press Limited
543/2 Castlehill
The Royal Mile
Edinburgh EH1 2ND
Scotland
Telephone: 0131 225 4326 (24 hours)
Fax: 0131 225 4324
email: gavin.macdougall@luath.co.uk
Website: www.luath.co.uk